T0137513

ONE THOUSAND YEARS

The Bright Side of Prophecy

DAVID COLEMAN

This book is a work of non-fiction. Unless otherwise noted, the author and the publisher make no explicit guarantees as to the accuracy of the information contained in this book and in some cases, names of people and places have been altered to protect their privacy.

WestBow Press books may be ordered through booksellers or by contacting:

WestBow Press
A Division of Thomas Nelson & Zondervan
1663 Liberty Drive
Bloomington, IN 47403
www.westbowpress.com
1 (866) 928-1240

ISBN: 978-1-9736-7936-3 (sc)
ISBN: 978-1-9736-7937-0 (hc)
ISBN: 978-1-9736-7935-6 (e)

Library of Congress Control Number: 2019918287

Print information available on the last page.

WestBow Press rev. date: 12/09/2019

For
Lee Ann, the love of my life

Contents

Acknowledgments xi
Introduction xiii

Chapter 1 Why the Millennium? 1

- Reason 1: To Bring Praise to the Father 2
- Reason 2: To Honor God's Covenants 3
  - God's Covenant with Abraham 4
  - The Palestinian Covenant 7
  - God's Covenant with David 8
  - The New Covenant 9
- Reason 3: To fulfill Prophecy 11
- Reason 4: To Conquer God's Enemies 12
- Reason 5: To Restore Israel and Make It Head of the Nations 13
- Reason 6: To Reward Old and New Testament Saints 14

Chapter 2 Launch of the Millennium 16

- Satan Bound 20
- Resurrection of Old Testament Saints and Tribulation Saints 21
- Millennial Preparations 22
- Regathering and Judgment of Israel 23
- Judgment of the Gentiles 24

Groundbreaking for the Millennial Temple...............25
Tribulation Cleanup...............26
Marriage Supper of the Lamb...............28
Residents of the Millennium...............29

Chapter 3 Life in the New World...............32

Back to Earth...............35
Features of the New World...............35
Satan Gone...............36
Society Permeated by Righteousness...............36
Partial Phaseout of the Curse...............37
A Stunning Makeover...............41
Israel Glorified...............42
A New Ethic for Business and Commerce...............45
Peace, Not War...............47
Human Life Spans in Israel Greatly Extended...............48
Tares among the Wheat...............50

Chapter 4 Christ's Government in the Millennium...............54

Christ's Rule over the Earth...............55
A Stern Ruler...............57
Resistance Is Futile...............59
Saints of State...............62
Israel's Role in Christ's Millennial Government...............66
Looking for That Blessed Hope...............69

Chapter 5 You in the Millennium...............71

A Perfect You...............72
Your New Nature...............77
Your Abilities...............78
Your Relationships...............79

Chapter 6 Worship in the Millennium 83

Full Disclosure 84
Undistracted Worship 87
Illumination by the Holy Spirit 87
Israel's Worship in the Millennium 88
Sabbath Observance (Ezekiel 44:1–3; 46:1–3) 89
Passover and the Feast of Unleavened Bread 90
The Feast of Tabernacles (Leviticus 23:33–36; Zechariah 14:16–17) 92
New Moon Observance (Numbers 10:10) 94

Chapter 7 Ezekiel's Troublesome Temple 96

Ezekiel's Temple 97
Objection #1: Ezekiel's Temple should be understood as an allegory designed to illustrate spiritual truths, rather than as an actual physical structure. 98
Objection #2: Ezekiel's description of the topography around the temple does not match that of Jerusalem today. 99
Objection #3: Ezekiel's mention of animal sacrifices offered in the temple (Ezekiel 43:18–27) conflicts with the New Testament's teaching that Christ was the ultimate and final sacrifice for sin. 100
Objection #4: The requirement of circumcision as a condition of entrance into the temple (Ezekiel 44:8) belongs to the Old Covenant rather than to the new. 106
Prince Who? 106

Chapter 8 The Eternal State 109

The Curse Repealed Entirely 113
Evil and Unrighteousness Banished 115
God the Father Acknowledged as Supreme 115
God the Father Reunited with His People 116
Continuation and Expansion of Millennial Blessings 118

Chapter 9 When the Perfect Comes 120

Eternally Fulfilling Relationships 122
Eternal Enjoyment of Beauty 122
Home Forever 124
Perfect Holiness 126

Bibliography 131
Endnotes 141

Acknowledgments

I wish to acknowledge my sincere gratitude to some very special people who helped make the writing of this book a possibility. Pastors are notoriously busy creatures, and without their support, I could not have made room in my life for such an undertaking. First, I wish to thank my wife, Lee Ann, for graciously permitting me to disappear into my study on many evenings to do research and to write. I am grateful to Ricky Bennett, a member of our church, for proofreading and editing the manuscript, and to Gary Fabian, our church's worship and administration pastor, for his help in researching hymns. May the Lord reward them both for their time and efforts. Last, I wish to express my appreciation to the members of Crowfield Baptist Church for granting me a sabbatical so that I could begin writing. Their gift of time enabled me to get this project underway in earnest.

Introduction

"Noise makes news."

According to Paul Harvey, the legendary radio broadcaster, that is the reason why American media outlets intentionally report mostly bad news. Good news just doesn't sell as well. In a lecture Harvey gave at Kansas State University, he said his own network, ABC, once produced a program featuring only good news, but it lasted only thirteen weeks because of low ratings.[1] Evidently, a majority of readers in the United States would agree with science fiction writer Arthur C. Clark, who wrote, "The newspapers of Utopia … would be terribly dull."[2] We find bad news much more exciting.

That may offer a clue as to why so many Christians today seem better acquainted with the Bible's apocalyptic revelations of the world's future than with the more upbeat events God says lie ahead. Handed pen and paper, many believers could probably write out relatively well-informed descriptions of end-time topics such as the Tribulation, the Antichrist, and the Battle of Armageddon, but many of those same believers might draw a blank if asked to give specifics about the future one-thousand-year age when Jesus will rule the earth as King of kings, generally known as the Millennium. Such unfamiliarity with that monumentally glorious age to come exposes a regrettable blind spot suffered by many Christians today, and it indicates that Paul Harvey's glum evaluation of human nature may have been spot-on.

The Bible foretells that, at the conclusion of the Great Tribulation,

Christ will return and set up an everlasting kingdom on earth. Believers from every age of human history will reign with Christ on the earth, blessed with total freedom from sin, suffering, and death. Even better, the entire world at that time will acknowledge Jesus Christ as King of kings. In light of that dazzlingly bright picture of what lies ahead for God's people, I find it perplexing that the lion's share of attention given to the study of eschatology by Christian preachers and writers today centers upon the dark and dreadful aspects of earth's future. Granted, much of this coverage is intended to shock unbelievers out of numbness to the Gospel, but let's not get lost in the dark.

Playing into this uneven treatment of prophetic events is the public's current obsession with the prospect of doomsday, which reflects the cynicism and growing despair that characterize our times. Television networks feature programs that explore every conceivable scenario of global disaster. The Sci-Fi Channel's 2006 documentary, *Countdown to Doomsday*, hosted by Matt Lauer, considered ten earth-threatening situations, including a supervolcano, an asteroid impact, a global pandemic, nuclear annihilation, mass rebellion by robots, and others. One observer commented, "In contemporary culture, utopia has all but disappeared from our imaginative map while dystopias proliferate."[3] In stark contrast to all this pessimism and preoccupation with catastrophe, the Bible shines a beacon of hope into humankind's despair by forecasting a magnificent future for God's redeemed people. My goal for this book is to shed some desperately needed light on that neglected area of eschatology (theologian's term for end-times prophecy). I want you to become acquainted with the bright side of biblical prophecy!

Several years ago on a Sunday morning at our church, I preached a sermon on the thousand-year reign of Christ. After spending hours the previous week poring over what the Bible reveals about that glorious time following Christ's Second Coming, I approached the pulpit mentally saturated with scriptural truth about it. Just before I stood to preach, our congregation sang the song "Let Your Glory

Fall" by Don Moen, which envisions Christ seated on His throne in Jerusalem during the Millennium, surrounded by adoring saints:

> Every tongue and tribe,
> Gathered 'round Your throne.
> With one voice we cry,
> Holy Lord …
> Glory to the Lamb,
> Lamb upon the throne … [4]

When I approached the pulpit after the song and began to lead the church in prayer, I became so overcome by the thought of Christ being worshipped by all peoples of the earth that I had to choke back tears. At that moment, the Millennium became one of my favorite subjects in Scripture, and it remains so today. In the years since, my fascination with the future time when "the earth will be full of the knowledge of the LORD as the waters cover the sea" (Isaiah 11:9) has not diminished but has intensified and deepened.

Try for a moment to imagine Jesus present bodily upon earth, ruling over a kingdom that encompasses the entire planet. At that time, no rational person will deny that Christ is God or reject His authority. All rebellion will meet with quick retribution, and absolute justice will prevail throughout the world. Righteousness will triumph over evil everywhere, and God's glory will extend from Jerusalem to the ends of the earth. All human beings who will have ever lived throughout history and who will have been reconciled to God by faith will live on the earth from that point throughout eternity, made perfect, and reigning with Jesus forever in His earthly kingdom.

When I began searching the Bible for references to the Millennium, I found far more of them than I expected. I discovered that at least twenty-nine books in both testaments and at least 127 chapters of Scripture make mention of it—and thirteen chapters focus upon it exclusively! I also began to realize Christian music through the centuries has proclaimed the Millennium in countless hymns and songs. It became obvious to me that all Christendom reverberates with the blessed news the Millennium.

Having become so captivated, I met with disappointment when I found most books on the Millennium are either scholarly works intended for seminarians or tomes written to defend this or that view of the Millennium. To my knowledge, relatively few writers have undertaken to expound the rich body of truth contained in Scripture that reveals what will occur in the Millennium and what everyday life in it will be like. I look forward to bringing these fascinating details out into the light of day.

If you are a believer in Christ, I offer you this book with the hope it will profoundly encourage you. I want to lead you on a tour of the magnificent earthly kingdom Christ will inaugurate upon His return, and in which you will live not only during the Millennium but forever. We will look as deeply as Scripture permits into that future time when Jesus rules as King of kings from His throne in Jerusalem, ensconced in heavenly glory. In that day, believers from throughout the ages will return from heaven in glorified supernatural bodies to rule over the kingdom under Christ's headship. Eden-like conditions will be restored in the Holy Land, and the nation of Israel will bless the entire human race in extraordinary ways. In Israel, if not throughout the world, human life spans will be dramatically extended, and predatory animals will become docile plant eaters and will coexist peacefully with other animals and with humans. Even the cosmos will undergo dramatic changes, all for the betterment of life on earth. What a wonderful time for God's redeemed people to look forward to!

To be sure, not everything we might wish to know about the Millennium is revealed in Scripture, and throughout this book, I will seek to avoid, or at least minimize, speculation. Still, Scripture does provide enough information—far more than I think many Christians realize—to enable us to piece together a fairly detailed sketch of life on earth then. As that sketch takes shape in the following pages, you may find yourself echoing longingly, as I have, the concluding words of Scripture, written by the apostle John: "Come Lord Jesus" (Revelation 22:20).

Two key questions of eschatology (the study of last things) focus upon the precise nature of the Millennium and its placement on God's end-time calendar, and attempts to answer these questions have led to sharp disagreement among interpreters throughout church history. Is the Millennium a literal period of earth history, and will it occur before or after Christ's Second Coming? Three major views in this debate have arisen through the centuries, and a brief summary of these views will help clarify my own perspective.

Premillennialism teaches that Christ will return prior to the Millennium. Most of the early church fathers from the second through the fourth centuries were premillennialists. Of the three positions on this question, this one takes the most literal view and sees the Millennium as an actual earthly reign of one thousand years (based upon Revelation 20:1–6). Over against this view stands *postmillennialism*, which teaches Christ will not return until after the Millennium. Interpreters who hold this view do not see the Millennium as a literal thousand-year age but rather as an indeterminate span of time in which universal peace and righteousness will characterize the world. They believe this period will be ushered in by a steady expansion of the Gospel, until all nations eventually turn to Christ.

Distinct from both of these views, *amillennialism* (*a* meaning "no") teaches all references to the Millennium in Scripture are purely figurative and should be understood as spiritualized descriptions of the rule of Christ in believers' hearts. They believe the Second Coming will be followed by a general resurrection of believers and unbelievers, after which will come the Last Judgment and, finally, the eternal state.

While I realize that sincere believers can be found within each of these interpretive camps, I believe premillennialism offers by far the best understanding of Scripture because of its reliance upon better principles of interpretation and because it more closely aligns with the views of the early church than do the other two systems. Postmillennialists and amillennialists base their views, to one extent or another, upon nonliteral, spiritualized understandings of end-time events, which is a highly subjective method of interpretation that leaves the interpreter free to impose upon any text whatever meaning they happen to prefer. As Paul Benware rightly observes, "When such spiritualizing or allegorizing takes place, the interpretation is no longer grounded in fact, and the text becomes putty in the hand of the interpreter."[5]

A distinctive component of premillennialism is its insistence that God has not abandoned Israel and that the Jews remain His chosen people today. God's covenants with Abraham and his descendants, and with David, require literal fulfillment in an earthly kingdom in order to bear any objective meaning. In His covenant with Abraham and the people of Israel (Genesis 17:1–14), God says, "'The whole land of Canaan … I will give as an everlasting possession to you and your descendants after you; and I will be their God'" (verse 8). Scripture clearly and repeatedly declares the Abrahamic Covenant will never be nullified.

In Psalm 105:8–11, the psalmist says of God: "He remembers his covenant forever, the word he commanded, for a thousand generations, the covenant he made with Abraham, the oath he swore to Isaac. He confirmed it to Jacob as a decree, to Israel as an everlasting covenant: 'To you I will give the land of Canaan as the portion you will inherit.'"

Similarly, in God's covenant with David (2 Samuel 7:10–17), God promises David that, out of his descendants, God will establish an eternal kingdom. He declares, "'Your house and your kingdom will endure forever before me; your throne will be established forever'" (v. 16). God said in Jeremiah 31:27–31 that He would make a New Covenant with Israel and that He would never reject the Jews as His chosen people, and Christ later ratified that covenant at the Last Supper. All these promises point with crystal clarity to a literal, earthly kingdom. As John MacArthur states, "The streams of the Abrahamic, Davidic, and New Covenants find their confluence in the millennial kingdom ruled over by the Messiah."[6]

Contrary to some interpreters who teach that God has replaced Israel with the New Testament Church (a view known as Replacement Theology or Supercessionism), the apostle Paul writes of the Jewish people in Romans 9:4, "Theirs is the adoption as sons; theirs the divine glory, the covenants, the receiving of the law, the temple worship and the promises." Paul's use of the present tense ("is" rather than "was") clearly shows that God's covenantal relationship with Israel will endure forever.

A literal understanding of the Millennium results from a natural, unbiased reading of descriptive statements about it found scattered throughout Scripture, such as Psalm 22:27–28 in which David foresees a time of global spiritual awakening when "all the ends of the earth will remember and turn to the LORD, and all the families of the nations will bow down before him." If David's statement is intended to be understood nonliterally, on what basis are we to know that it does? And if it is symbolic, then what exactly does it symbolize? All attempts to answer such questions are nothing but sophistry and guesswork.

Finally, when the prophet Daniel interpreted Nebuchadnezzar's dream in Daniel 2, in verse 44 Daniel says to the Babylonian king, "'the God of heaven will set up a kingdom that will never be destroyed, nor will it be left to another people. It will crush all those kingdoms and bring them to an end, but it will itself endure forever.'" Daniel's announcement comes within his literal interpretation of Nebuchadnezzar's vision, and so the announcement itself clearly cannot be taken as symbolic or allegorical.

"When the natural sense makes sense, seek no other sense." This and other basic rules of grammatical-historical interpretation lead the student of Scripture to expect nothing other than a literal, earthly millennial kingdom, ruled over by the Lord Jesus Christ.[7]

Conventional laws of grammar and logic in Scripture interpretation lead to no other view.

When you study all that the Bible reveals about planet Earth's future, the Millennium shines like a brilliant jewel against the gloom of the Tribulation period that will come before it. The more you discover about the Millennium, the more anxiously you will anticipate its arrival. No serious student of biblical prophecy would deny that dark days lie ahead for this world. However, the Christian should bear in mind Christ's reassuring words in John 16:33, spoken to His disciples at the Last Supper: "In this world you will have trouble. But take heart! I have overcome the world."

So join me on an expedition into the grandest era our planet will have ever known. Peer with me through the telescope of Scripture to see what wonderful things God has in store for this world in times to come. A hundred years ago, a Swiss historian named Jakob Burckhardt wrote, "Neither in the life of the individual nor in that of mankind is it desirable to know the future."

I must disagree!

I

Why the Millennium?

> Such a future age of blessing, peace, and glory constitutes one of the great Bible doctrines and is in reality the great hope of the world, the hope of all hopes.
>
> —Arno C. Gaebelein[8]

If God were to put you in charge of planning His prophetic calendar, would you skip the Millennium? Maybe you would prefer to transition from Christ's Second Coming straight into eternity. After all, is a one-thousand-year interval between the Second Coming and eternity really necessary? Why not launch into the new heavens and new earth as soon as Jesus sets foot upon the Mount of Olives? These are reasonable questions, and, thankfully, we don't have to resort to speculation in order to answer them. All we need to do is go to the Scriptures.

As you read and reflect upon the entire witness of Scripture regarding the Millennium, you will begin to realize that most of the Bible would be pointless without the thousand-year reign of Christ. Without it, many of God's great promises could never be kept, and a slew of biblical prophecies would go unfulfilled forever. Bypassing Christ's earthly reign would sabotage God's plan for the nation of

Israel, and far worse, it would cheat Christ out of what the Father promised Him when He said to His Son, "Ask of me, and I will make the nations your inheritance, the ends of the earth your possession" (Psalm 2:8). For these reasons and others, the Millennium simply must happen!

To fully grasp the Millennium's tremendous significance to God's eternal plan, we must survey six distinct yet interwoven reasons for it. These reasons form a rock-solid case for why our world's timeline must include a literal thousand-year earthly reign of Jesus Christ, sometimes referred to by Bible students as the eschaton—the final event on God's prophetic calendar.

Reason 1: To Bring Praise to the Father

Throughout Scripture, we are told God's ultimate purpose for what He does is to bring glory to Himself (Exodus 14:17–18; 1 Samuel 12:22; 2 Samuel 7:23; Psalm 106:7–8; Isaiah 48:9–11; Isaiah 49:3; Romans 9:17; Ephesians 1:4–6). Bible teachers often express this truth by saying God exists for His own glory. Or as pastor and author John Piper puts it, the glory of God is the goal of history. From the beginning of creation, God has displayed His glory by demonstrating His holiness, His wisdom, and His power. God works in history to prove that He alone is God and is exclusively worthy of His creatures' adoration and praise.

Thomas Manton, a seventeenth-century Puritan clergyman, directly connected God's glory with the Millennium when he wrote, "[God's] glory is the great end, and the coming of his kingdom is the first and primary means. For God's glory is more manifest in his kingdom than in any other of his works."[9] In other words, Christ's millennial kingdom will display God's glory more fully and profoundly than anything else God has done in history.

God will use the Millennium to demonstrate His worthiness to receive humankind's worship and praise in ways that are impossible under the present world order that is dominated by Satan, whom the apostle Paul described as "the ruler of the kingdom of the air, the spirit who is now at work in those who are disobedient" (Ephesians 2:2). At the Second Coming, Christ will confine Satan to the Abyss, where he will remain throughout the Millennium. And Christ will establish His kingdom and will rule over the entire earth forever. In writing to the Thessalonian church, the apostle Paul said Christ will return "to be glorified in his holy people, and to be marveled at among all who have believed" (2 Thessalonians 1:9–10). Here Paul clearly identifies Christ's glory as a pivotal reason for His millennial kingdom. Throughout the Millennium, the glory of God and of Christ will dominate human existence on earth, "for the earth will be filled with the knowledge of the glory of the Lord as the waters cover the sea" (Habakkuk 2:14).

Reason 2: To Honor God's Covenants

The Millennium will serve as God's ultimate demonstration of His faithfulness to do what He says He will do and fulfill all His purposes. The eschaton will verify beyond all question the genuineness of God's sovereignty and trustworthiness. This is declared by God Himself in Isaiah 46:9–11, where He says,

> "I am God, and there is no other; I am God, and there is none like me. I make known the end from the beginning, from ancient times, what is still to come. I say: My purpose will stand, and I will do all that I please. … What I have said, that will I bring about; what I have planned, that will I do."

The Millennium will bring the fulfillment of all of God's historic covenants that are unfulfilled, some of which He made with specific individuals, others with the nation of Israel, and still others with all humanity.

In the Bible, a covenant is an agreement entered into by two parties in which each promises to abide by the terms of the covenant for the achievement of some mutually agreed-upon benefit or purpose. Covenants differ from contracts primarily in that covenants are based upon trust and good faith, whereas contracts are based upon law and suspicion. Of the seven covenants found in the Bible,[10] the Millennium will bring about the fulfillment of four in particular. It should be noted that of the covenants recorded in the Pentateuch (the first five books of the Bible), God's covenant with Noah, known as the Noahic Covenant, stands apart from the others by way of its application to all humanity and its pertinence to a particular form of judgment (a worldwide flood), while the other covenants are exclusively between God and the Israelites. Therefore, we will not include that covenant in our rundown of purposes for the Millennium.

God's Covenant with Abraham

Of major importance to the Millennium is the covenant God made with Abraham (Genesis 12:1–3 and 15:18–21) for the simple reason that it lays the foundation for all of God's plans for Israel that will be fulfilled during it. God promised Abraham He would give him and his descendants the land of Canaan, thus referred to as "the Promised Land" (Hebrews 11:9), by which it has been known for two millennia to millions of believers the world over. God even specified the exact borders of the land He would give them so there would be no mistake. Again and again in Scripture, God reiterated His promise concerning the land, using language like "everlasting," "forever," and "throughout all generations" to emphasize it would never be revoked under any circumstances. Thus, we can be sure the nation of Israel must possess their homeland forever if God's integrity is to be trusted.

To further confirm its perpetuity, God ratified His covenant with Abraham in an extraordinary way. Covenants are entered into mutually by two consenting parties, and most covenants in biblical times required each party to keep their end of the bargain, or the agreement would be rendered null and void. But God set up His covenant with Abraham in such a way that it was entirely one-sided on God's part, meaning God would honor His promises *whether or not* Abraham and his descendants—the Jews—remained faithful to Him.

In Genesis 12, when Abraham was seventy-five years old, God called him to leave his ancestral home in Ur—modern Iraq—and to relocate to the land of Canaan. God promised Abraham that He would bless him abundantly and multiply his descendants into a great nation. Then, some twenty-five years later, Genesis 15 records that God repeated this promise to Abraham and ratified it with a formal covenant.

Just before sunset one day, and following the customary form of Chaldean land grant treaties of the time, God instructed Abraham to gather several animal carcasses for sacrifice. He had Abraham cut some of the carcasses into halves and place the halves opposite each other on an altar. Abraham must have assumed that he and God would then participate together in the common ritual of ratifying the covenant by walking between the sacrifices as each promised to keep the terms of the covenant. However, as night approached, God caused Abraham to fall into a deep sleep, and then God walked *alone* between the sacrifices while saying to Abraham, "To your descendants I give this land" (Genesis 15:17–18).

God thereby established a unilateral and unconditional covenant with Abraham and his descendants. He obligated Himself to honor the covenant forever, regardless of whether Abraham and the Jews lived in obedience to him or not. As Mitch and Zhava Glaser note,

> For some sovereign reason unknown to us, God chose to love the Jewish people and through this

> nation to express His love for the world … What was Israel's mission? To proclaim to the world the God of Israel is the only true God and there is no other Savior but He.[11]

This fact is vital to understanding the significance of the Abrahamic Covenant to the literal fulfillment of the Millennium.

It is also important for us to know that Abraham and his descendants received ownership of the land of Israel at the moment the covenant was made. God essentially gave Israel the title deed to the Promised Land at the ratification ceremony, and the land has remained their property ever since. God did not say to Abraham, "I *will* give you this land." He said to him, "I *give* this land" (Genesis 15:18). God bequeathed the land to them on the spot, then and there, and Israel's ownership of the land was thus established forever.

Today, the nation of Israel occupies most but not all of the land God gave them in His covenant with Abraham, but during the Millennium, Israel will permanently occupy every square foot of it. This must happen, for anything less would constitute a breach of promise on God's part. Therefore, the Millennium is absolutely essential to the fulfillment of the Abrahamic Covenant.

In the Millennium, God will demonstrate His absolute faithfulness to keep His promises by fully honoring His covenant with Abraham and his descendants. Against overwhelming odds, God will see to it that the Jewish people will live in their ancestral homeland for eternity.

Some interpreters of Scripture dismiss Israel's eternal possession of the Promised Land on the purported grounds the biblical writers themselves never envisioned the Millennium as literal but as only symbolic of various spiritual realities, or on the notion that God's millennial promises to Israel were voided by Israel's unbelief. Adherents of replacement theology argue that God has supplanted Israel with the church and that national Israel no longer has any role to play in God's eternal plan. These views are nothing short of outrageous in light of the clear-cut language of God's covenant with Abraham and his descendants.

While it is true that Israel forfeited its land through disobedience and was temporarily set aside by God as a result (Matthew 21:43; Romans 11:1–26), Scripture declares that God will not abandon His people forever. As prophecy expert Mark Hitchcock points out, "God promised to bring the Jewish people to salvation and to fulfill His good promise that they will one day have ownership of the land forever."[12] We may be certain God will keep His covenant with Abraham and that He will be glorified for His faithfulness in doing so.

The Palestinian Covenant

Another covenant God will fulfill in the Millennium is the covenant He made with the Israelites at the conclusion of their wandering in the wilderness during the Exodus. Known as the Palestinian Covenant or Land Covenant, it reiterated and expanded the covenant God made with Abraham some seven hundred years earlier, and, like the Abrahamic Covenant, it is unconditional and eternal.

In Deuteronomy 30:1–10, Moses records that, shortly before the Israelites crossed the Jordan River to take possession of the land, God foretold they would sin against Him and He would cast them out of the Promised Land, but that they would then repent, and He would later regather them in the land and bless them abundantly. Afterward, those things did happen, exactly as He said. When we fast-forward to today, we find nearly everything in Scripture God foretold would happen to Israel has already been literally fulfilled in history, and there is therefore no reason to doubt that His promised millennial blessings upon Israel will also be fulfilled literally.

God's Covenant with David

In 2 Samuel 7:8–16, God made a covenant with King David, in which God reaffirmed His promise to permanently plant the Israelites in their homeland. In the Davidic Covenant, God also promised David that his descendants would rule over Israel forever. This did not mean members of David's dynasty would occupy the throne in an unbroken line but that, ultimately, a descendant of David would sit as king over Israel forever. In Luke 1:32–33, the angel Gabriel announced to Mary that her Son, whom she was to give the name Jesus, would be the literal fulfillment of that covenant:

> "He will be great and will be called the Son of the Most High. The Lord God will give him the throne of his father David, and he will reign over the house of Jacob forever; his kingdom will never end."

As with the Abrahamic Covenant, God's covenant with David is eternal (2 Samuel 7:13; Psalm 89:3–4, 28–37). It is also unconditional, according to God's unmistakable language when He said, "I will maintain my love to [David] forever, and my covenant with him will never fail" (Psalm 89:28). God declared that nothing could ever cause Him to renege on His promise to preserve David's dynasty "as long as the heavens endure" (Psalm 89:29). Thus, the Davidic Covenant guarantees an earthly kingdom in which an heir of David will occupy the throne of Israel forever.[13] That heir is Jesus Christ, whose ancestry traces back to David through both Joseph and Mary (Matthew 1:1–17; Luke 3:23–31).

Amillennialists, who deny the literality of the Millennium, claim that Jesus has already fulfilled God's promise to David by occupying His throne in heaven as head of the church. Numerous problems reveal that notion to be pure sophistry, including the fact that such a "spiritualized" interpretation flies in the face of the covenant's wording that is clearly intended to be understood literally (2 Samuel 7:8–16). David would surely have understood it literally, having no reason to take it any other way. Furthermore, anything short of a literal fulfillment of the covenant would render God's promises in it concerning Israel's ancestral homeland utterly meaningless. The millennial kingdom of Christ will prove God is faithful to His covenant with David, and it will confirm God's holiness (Psalm 89:34–37). Jesus will sit on the throne of Israel, and all who are in heaven and on earth will glorify God for His sovereignty and trustworthiness.

The New Covenant

A final covenant that requires a literal Millennium in order for it to be fulfilled is the New Covenant God said He would establish with Israel and with Judah in Jeremiah 31:31–34. This covenant is not about land or dynasties but about the spiritual regeneration of the Jewish people. In it, God promised to bring about a future spiritual awakening in which the entire Jewish race will come to faith in Him. It assures that all Jews living in the Millennium will belong to God by faith.

> "The time is coming," declares the LORD, "when I will make a new covenant with the house of Israel and with the house of Judah. It will not be like the covenant I made with their forefathers when I took them by the hand to lead them out of Egypt, because they broke my covenant, though I was a husband to them," declares the LORD. "This is the covenant I will make with the house of Israel after that time," declares the LORD. "I will put my law in their minds and write it on their hearts. I will be their God, and they will be my people. No longer will a man teach His neighbor, or a man His brother, saying, 'Know the LORD,' because they

> will all know me, from the least of them to the greatest," declares the LORD. "For I will forgive their wickedness and will remember their sins no more." (Jeremiah 31:31–34)

The New Covenant will be fulfilled in the millennial kingdom when all Israel comes to faith in Christ. Today, all believers, including Gentiles, participate in the blessings of the New Covenant, but the covenant itself was specifically made by God with Israel (the "houses" of Israel and Judah will be reunited into one people and nation in the millennial age). At no time in history have 100 percent of the Jewish people—or any other race—been in right relationship with God. Today, the overwhelming majority of Jews do not accept Jesus as their Messiah, but their rejection will give way to acceptance of Him in the Millennium. Christ will cause every Jew who enters His kingdom to do so as a born-again believer, and this epic conversion and regeneration of the Jews will bring glory and praise to God.

Premillennialists call these four covenants "determinative" because they establish a fixed outcome for Israel's future. As we have seen, each of these covenants is unconditional and one-sided on God's part. As such, each covenant also serves as a litmus test of God's faithfulness to keep His word. In all four covenants, God obligated Himself to keep specific promises to the Jewish people regardless of what they do or fail to do. Although the Jewish people have forfeited many blessings they could otherwise have enjoyed throughout their history had they not rebelled against God, the essential promises contained in the covenants remain in effect.

We can therefore see that the language and content of God's covenants call for a literal earthly kingdom in order for them to make sense and to find complete fulfillment. In the Millennium, God will keep all of His remaining covenantal promises that will not have been fulfilled prior to that time. As a result, all who are on earth and in heaven will praise God for His faithfulness, and His glory will be greatly heightened.

Reason 3: To fulfill Prophecy

God displays His sovereignty in a major way through the fulfillment of prophecy, because His power becomes evident when His prophecies come to pass exactly as He issues them. God alone predetermines future outcomes, and He alone can reveal events before they happen (Isaiah 46:9–10). In contrast, unfulfilled predictions expose false prophets as frauds and con artists (Deuteronomy 18:22).

Fulfilled prophecy also demonstrates that God can do whatever He wants and His plans cannot be thwarted. God can even use even His enemies to fulfill His purposes, and He has often done so. As John Piper says, "The enemies of God do not frustrate God's decrees; they execute them."[14] All of the major prophets (Isaiah, Jeremiah, Ezekiel, and Daniel) foresaw and heralded the Millennium, as did all of the twelve minor prophets, except Jonah. With so much attention given in Scripture to Christ's millennial kingdom, its literal fulfillment will affirm God's greatness conclusively and His exclusive worthiness of worship and praise.

Notice how God Himself emphasizes His glory in connection with events of the Millennium:

> "And I … am about to come and gather all nations and tongues, and they will come and see *my glory.* I will set a sign among them, and I will send some of those who survive to the nations … and to the distant islands that have not heard of my fame or seen *my glory.* They will proclaim *my glory* among the nations." (Isaiah 66:18–19)

Another effect of fulfilled prophecy is its verification of the inspiration of Scripture, for how could the Bible's hundreds of predictions come true with such amazing accuracy unless they were, in fact, uttered by God? Over one-fourth of the Bible is made up of predictive prophecy, and each and every foretelling of a future event put God's credibility on the line. The failure of just one prophecy to come true would seriously impugn God's sovereignty and the credibility of the Scriptures. On the other hand, each instance in which something God foretold in Scripture does come to pass further underscores the genuineness and veracity of all of God's Word, and Christ's millennial kingdom will serve as the consummate tribute to the absolute trustworthiness of Scripture and of its Author.

Reason 4: To Conquer God's Enemies

The Millennium will bring about the final defeat of all God's enemies, including Satan and the demons and all humans who reject Him. Numerous Scriptures in both the Old and the New Testaments attest to this outcome (Psalm 2:8–12; Revelation 2:26–27; 12:4–5; 19:15).

Mortal human beings, both saved and lost, will live on earth in the Millennium. We will explore this feature of millennial life in greater detail later. At the Millennium's outset, all mortal human beings alive on earth will be believers in Christ, and because they will exist in earthly bodies, they will be capable of producing offspring. Some of their children will refuse to turn to Christ for salvation, and they will demonstrate their unbelief by rebelling against Christ's authority. However, Christ will maintain zero tolerance for rebellion, and He will bring swift judgment upon all who disobey Him—even upon entire nations (Zechariah 14:17–18).

Scripture reveals that, near the conclusion of the Millennium, Satan will be released once again and will "go out to deceive the nations in the four corners of the earth" (Revelation 20:7–8). Many believers find it baffling that God will release Satan from captivity, but it will serve the purpose of irrefutably exposing human depravity, because unbelievers alive at that time will choose to rebel against Christ and follow Satan, despite having lived under Christ's benevolent rule. Prompted by Satan, hordes of unbelievers will mount a final assault upon Jerusalem where Christ sits enthroned as King, but Christ will call down fire from heaven and destroy them, and He will immediately cast Satan into the lake of fire forever. Christ will then sentence all unbelievers who will have ever lived to eternal damnation at the Great White Throne Judgment, and He will cast them into the lake of fire, where they will suffer eternal punishment along with Satan and his demons.

During the Millennium, Christ will conquer all of His enemies wherever they exist and purge evil from every corner of creation. Thus, at the outset of the eternal state following the Millennium, the New Jerusalem will arrive in a fresh new world that is entirely and forever free of sin and evil, a world solely occupied by God and His redeemed people, whom J. I. Packer describes as "a vast perfected society."[15] God's glory will be displayed in all its grand fullness, and He will be praised by the angels and by glorified believers throughout eternity. Reminiscent of the typical fairy-tale ending, they will live happily ever after.

Reason 5: To Restore Israel and Make It Head of the Nations

The Millennium is largely about Israel. In the eschaton, God will fulfill every one of His promises made to Abraham and his descendants, the Jews. In Psalm 102:13, the writer sums up every blessing God will bestow upon Israel in the millennial age in one sentence: "You will arise and have compassion on Zion, for it is time to show favor to her; the appointed time has come." Millions of Jews throughout history have longed for that promise to come true. At Passover each year, the Jewish Seder ends with the phrase, "Next year in Jerusalem"[16]—an expression of the Jewish yearning for the Messiah to come and rebuild Jerusalem and the temple. This ancient hope will become reality for converted Jews when Jesus returns and establishes His earthly kingdom.

God will shower the land of Israel with extraordinary blessings in the millennial age, and He will make Israel the premier nation of the world. Christ will establish His throne in Jerusalem, thereby making it the earth's capital city and its religious, cultural, and economic center. Israel will enjoy unprecedented global prominence and prosperity. As a result, all of the world's nations will be forced to acknowledge God's favor upon Israel and His making her "the praise of the earth" (Isaiah 62:6–7).

Reason 6: To Reward Old and New Testament Saints

God loves to bless His people for their faithfulness, and in the millennial kingdom, He will lavishly reward all believers who will have lived throughout history for their acts of obedience and service. Isaiah 40:10 pictures Christ at the Second Coming and says "the Sovereign LORD comes with power, and his arm rules for him. See, his *reward is with him*, and his recompense accompanies him." Conversely, Christ's "reward" for unbelievers will take the form of eternal damnation.

God will reward His saints primarily by placing them in positions of authority and leadership in His kingdom, a truth expressed in both the Old and New Testaments (Daniel 7:18–27; 1 Corinthians 6:2–3; Revelation 2:26–28; 20:4, 6). In the New Testament, God's rewards for believers are often described as crowns (1 Thessalonians 2:19; 2 Timothy 4:8; James 1:12; 1 Peter 5:4; Revelation 2:10). Crowns are appropriate because they illustrate the rulership Christ will grant believers in His kingdom in proportion to their obedience in this life. Much more will be said about this later.

When God fulfills all of His covenantal promises and accomplishes His purposes for world history, His supremacy will shine like the sun for all in heaven and on earth to see. While the world languishes during the Great Tribulation, God's redeemed ones in heaven will sing this song of triumph to the Lord: "'Great and marvelous are your deeds, Lord God Almighty. Just and true are your ways, King of the ages. Who will not fear you, O Lord, and bring glory to your name? For you alone are holy. All nations will come and worship before you, for your righteous acts have been revealed'" (Revelation 15:3–4). That declaration of nations coming to bow before the Lord will come true during the Millennium.

All of this enables us to see that deleting the Millennium from God's prophetic calendar would reduce human history to a cliff-hanger with no sequel, but God will not leave His work in the world unfinished. For all of the reasons we have presented in this chapter, the Millennium is absolutely necessary—and guaranteed! The Millennium will provide a context in which God will keep all of His promises to Israel and utterly crush His foes, and God will bring His plan for earth and humankind to its intended conclusion. It also will provide an earthly setting for Jesus Christ to be honored and glorified and worshipped as Lord, to the glory of God the Father. The Millennium is clearly the capstone of history.

2

Launch of the Millennium

> See, the Sovereign LORD comes with power, and his arm rules for him. See, his reward is with him, and his recompense accompanies him.
>
> —Isaiah 40:10

I once heard Charles Swindoll point out in a sermon that God's great eras in history always begin with a dramatic display of miracles. His observation certainly bears true of the Millennium, because Christ's Second Coming will set off a series of supernatural events that make way for the Millennium that will be unlike anything that has occurred since God created the earth. Most Christians know that when Jesus returns, He will defeat the Antichrist at the Battle of Armageddon and will bring the Great Tribulation to its close, but then what? Many believers have only a vague awareness of what the Bible says will take place after Christ returns. What events will follow our Lord's Second Coming, and how will Christ set up His earthly kingdom? To answer these questions, we must begin by looking at the event of Christ's return itself.

Several passages in the Bible describe Jesus's return and the world's reaction to His sudden appearance:

On that day his feet will stand on the Mount of Olives, east of Jerusalem, and the Mount of Olives will be split in two from east to west, forming a great valley, with half of the mountain moving north and half moving south. (Zechariah 14:4)

"For as lightning that comes from the east is visible even in the west, so will be the coming of the Son of Man. … At that time the sign of the Son of Man will appear in the sky, and all the nations of the earth will mourn. They will see the Son of Man coming on the clouds of the sky, with power and great glory." (Matthew 24:27, 30)

Look, he is coming with the clouds, and every eye will see him, even those who pierced him; and all the peoples of the earth will mourn because of him. So shall it be! Amen. (Revelation 1:7)

I saw heaven standing open and there before me was a white horse, whose rider is called Faithful and True. With justice he judges and makes war. His eyes are like blazing fire, and on his head are many crowns. He has a name written on him that no one knows but he himself. He is dressed in a robe dipped in blood, and his name is the Word of God. The armies of heaven were following him, riding on white horses and dressed in fine linen, white and clean. Out of his mouth comes a sharp sword with which to strike down the nations. "He will rule them with an iron scepter." He treads the winepress of the fury of the wrath of God Almighty. On his robe and on his thigh he has this name written:

> King of Kings and Lord of Lords. (Revelation 19:11–16)

Christ's Second Coming will change the world and alter the course of human history more drastically than any other event will have done since Adam and Eve were expelled from the Garden of Eden. For unbelievers, His return will bring terror and dread, because they will realize that Jesus is God and that they are utterly unprepared to face Him. They will instantly know how foolish they were for rejecting Christ and choosing to persist in unbelief, but it will be too late. No wonder the Bible says the people of earth will mourn because of Him!

In Revelation 19:11–21, the apostle John describes a vision shown to him by God in which he beholds Christ seated on a white horse, looking like a fierce warrior going forth to conquer. Following the Lord are "the armies of heaven" who also ride white horses and are "dressed in fine linen, white and clean" (v. 14). Some Bible interpreters believe the armies John saw are angels, but most likely they are redeemed human beings who have died and are returning from heaven with Christ. Hints in the text strongly suggest that this understanding is correct.

One indication of the armies' identity is seen in the clothing they are wearing. John says they are dressed in white linen, and earlier in John's vision, the "bride" of the Lamb, which is identified elsewhere in Scripture as the church (2 Corinthians 11:2; Ephesians 5:25–27), is given "fine linen, white and clean" to wear, which, John points out, "stands for the righteous acts of the saints." In the New Testament, fine linen is nearly always mentioned in conjunction with believers who are in heaven, so it would seem unlikely that these armies John sees are angels, but rather humans who will have put faith in Christ, then died and were taken to heaven.

Another hint is found in 1 Thessalonians 4:14, where Paul declares that, at the Second Coming, "God will bring with Jesus those who have fallen asleep in him," and in Revelation 17:14, which describes Christ's victory at Armageddon immediately after His return. An angel says, "with him will be his called, chosen and faithful followers." It seems reasonable, therefore, to identify these armies in John's vision as the souls of believers who have died throughout the centuries and who come with Christ to participate in His earthly kingdom.

When Christ returns, He will intervene in the Battle of Armageddon that will already be underway. This battle will begin when, for purposes not fully explained in Scripture, armies from around the world will gather in Israel, perhaps intending to eradicate the Jewish people once and for all. Jerusalem will have been recently attacked and captured, and its citizens brutalized. Then, suddenly and without warning, Christ will appear and stand on the Mount of Olives just outside Jerusalem (Zechariah 14:4), and this will trigger a massive geological upheaval that will dramatically alter the topography in and around Jerusalem. Christ will destroy the rebellious armies with nothing but "the breath of his mouth" (2 Thessalonians 2:8), and He will seize the Antichrist and the false prophet and cast them alive into the lake of fire. The entire region will become a scene of grisly carnage where hordes of birds come to feast on the corpses lying scattered over the landscape (Revelation 19:20–21).

Scripture does not explicitly say the saints in Christ's armies will be armed with any kind of weapons or that they will even take part in the fighting. Evidently, they will simply watch in astonishment as Jesus wins a series of swift and easy victories singlehandedly. At the end of the Battle of Armageddon, no one will remain who opposes Christ or His people. God's dreadful judgments poured out upon the world during the Tribulation will end, all warfare will cease, and Earth will be released from the domination of Satan and his minions and brought under the righteous rule of Christ. What a radical revolution that will be!

Satan Bound

In the Book of Revelation, chapter 20, the apostle John is given a vision in which he watches an angel take hold of Satan and cast him into the Abyss .[17] The context implies this will happen immediately after Christ's victory at Armageddon, recorded in Revelation 19. The exact location of the Abyss is not revealed in Scripture, but it would seem to be a place remote from the earth. John says the purpose for Satan's confinement will be "to keep him from deceiving the nations" (v. 3). As we have already pointed out, Satan will be released from the Abyss just prior to the end of the Millennium and will resume his work of deception for a brief time, and we will point out the reasons why God permits this later in this book.

Satan's removal from the earth prior to the Millennium will be necessary because no world peace or age of righteousness would be possible if Satan remained present. Satan is pictured throughout Scripture as a deceiver (Genesis 3:1–7; John 8:44; Revelation 20:7–8) and a tempter (Matthew 4:1–11; 1 Corinthians 7:5; 1 Thessalonians 3:5; Revelation 12:9). Satan's absence will result in a dramatic decrease in sin on the part of earth's mortal human inhabitants, although mortal humans will still possess a fallen nature that is prone to sin.

There is another reason why Satan must be removed from the world before Christ's reign can begin. When Satan rebelled against God and was cast out of heaven to the earth (Isaiah 14:12–15), the world became Satan's sphere of dominion, and he rules over unbelievers with a measure of provisional authority within bounds set for him by God. Therefore, he must be deposed and ousted in order for Christ to lay claim to the earth as King.

Satan's current reign over the world is acknowledged repeatedly in the New Testament. For example, Jesus did not dispute Satan's ability to grant Him rulership over the world's kingdoms when Satan tempted Him in the wilderness, nor did He deny Satan's claim that God had given him authority to do so (Luke 4:6). Later in His ministry, Christ acknowledged Satan's jurisdiction over the earth by calling him "the prince of this world" (John 12:31; 14:30; 16:11). The apostle Paul called Satan "the god of this age" (2 Corinthians 4:4) and "the ruler of the kingdom of the air" (Ephesians 2:2), and the apostle John said, "The whole world is under the control of the evil one" (1 John 5:19). Because of these realities, Satan absolutely must be banished from the earth before Christ's millennial kingdom can take place. Demons will undoubtedly also be removed from the earth at that time. A supernatural decontamination of the planet will take place! As Martin Luther declared in his triumphant hymn, "A Mighty Fortress is Our God":

> The Prince of Darkness grim, we tremble not for him;
> His rage we can endure, for lo, his doom is sure,
> One little word shall fell him.[18]

Resurrection of Old Testament Saints and Tribulation Saints

Multiple passages in Scripture point to a time when Old Testament believers will be raised to life (Job 19:25–27; Isaiah 26:19; Daniel 12:1–2; Hosea 13:14). In Daniel 12, their resurrection is foretold to occur after the "time of distress" (v. 1), which is an obvious reference to the Great Tribulation. Their resurrection will presumably occur in conjunction with the resurrection of believers who will have been martyred by the Antichrist's regime during the Tribulation.

According to the traditional pretribulational view, all Christians who will have died prior to the Rapture will be resurrected at the Rapture and taken to heaven, along with all Christians who are alive on the earth at that time. During the Tribulation, it will be possible for unbelievers to put faith in Christ and be saved, but many who do so will be martyred for their faith. The fact that conversion to Christ will be possible during the Tribulation is evidenced in Revelation 7:9–17 where John describes a "great multitude" of believers in heaven who "have come out of the great tribulation." No Christians who are saved prior to the Rapture will be on earth when the Tribulation begins, so this multitude could only have been saved during the Tribulation. They will remain in heaven until Christ's Second Coming, when their bodies will be resurrected and rejoined with their spirits, and they will then take part in the Millennium.

Prophecy expert and author John Walvoord says,

> These descriptions of the resurrections show that before the Millennium all the righteous dead will have been raised in one resurrection or another and will enter the millennial kingdom in their resurrection bodies. Only the wicked will remain in their graves to be subject to resurrection at the end of the millennial kingdom.[19]

Millennial Preparations

In Daniel 12:11-13, Scripture records a vision given to the prophet Daniel in which a "man clothed in linen" discloses a timeline for the period between the midpoint of the Tribulation and the start of the Millennium. This person, who was either an angel or the preincarnate Christ, says to Daniel, "From the time that the daily sacrifice is abolished and the abomination that causes desolation is set up, there will be 1,290 days." He then says, "Blessed is the one who waits for and reaches the end of the 1,335 days."

Because the second half of the Tribulation will last for 1,260 days (three and one-half years), the number of days the man announces reveals a seventy-five-day interval of time between the end of the Tribulation and the launch of the Millennium. Prophecy experts sometimes refer to this interval as an "interregnum." Why will it occur? Although it certainly is mysterious, when we consider that the Bible foretells several key transitional events that will take place after Christ's Second Coming and prior to the Millennium, we begin to realize that this interval of time will be necessary. Some interpreters have likened it to the span of time between a US president's election in November and his inauguration in January, during which preparations for their taking office are made. It is impossible to know the exact order in which these events will occur, but in the following paragraphs, I suggest one possible sequence.

Regathering and Judgment of Israel

God will use the terrible sufferings of the Tribulation to break the Jews' resistance to Christ as their Messiah and to lead vast numbers of them to saving faith. According to Zechariah 13:8–9, two-thirds of all Jews living in Israel during the Tribulation will be killed, but a large portion of the one-third who survive will be saved. This mass conversion of Jews will end the "times of the Gentiles" (Luke 21:24) and will prepare this Jewish remnant for entry into the Millennium so that God's many covenantal promises to national Israel can be fulfilled.

When Christ returns, He will bring together in one place all Jews from the four corners of the earth who survive the Tribulation in order to purge from among them those who are unsaved (Isaiah 11:11–12; Ezekiel 20:33–38). This judgment of Israel will take place in the "desert of the nations" (Ezekiel 20:35), which will probably be some remote location outside the borders of Israel, perhaps even Mt. Sinai where God first met with the Israelites after bringing them out of Egypt in the Exodus. John Walvoord says, "Though this [judgment] is not clearly to be identified with any locality, the comparison with the dealings of God with Israel on the way from Egypt to the promised land seems to indicate the judgment takes place just outside the area given to Israel for perpetual possession."[20] Whatever the exact location, Christ will determine then and there who among the surviving Jews are born again and are thus qualified to enter His millennial kingdom and who are not.

Judgment of the Gentiles

At that time, Christ will also determine who among the Gentile survivors of the Tribulation are redeemed. According to Joel 3:2, 12, their judgment, described by Jesus in Matthew 25:31–46, will take place in the Valley of Jehoshaphat, which probably refers to the Kidron Valley that runs along the eastern side of Jerusalem. It will then be called the Valley of Decision (Joel 3:14), and there, "all the nations" will be brought and made to stand before the Lord, who will be enthroned in glory. This event is often referred to as the Sheep-Goat Judgment, but it is best understood as the Judgment of the Gentiles, because the Greek word translated "nations" in some English versions is *ethna* and is used in the New Testament to denote Gentiles.

Jesus "'will separate the people one from another as a shepherd separates the sheep from the goats'" (Matthew 25:32). In ancient Palestine, sheep and goats would often graze together in daylight hours, but at night, the shepherds would separate them so the goats could be gathered into warm shelters, while the thicker-coated sheep slept in the open air. Jesus often referred to His followers as His sheep, signifying His loving care for them as their Good Shepherd.

After weeding out unbelievers from among His true saints, Christ will say to all of His people, Jews and Gentiles alike, "'Come, you who are blessed by my Father; take your inheritance, the kingdom prepared for you since the creation of the world'" (Matthew 25:34). Then they will be ushered as a group into Christ's kingdom, and unbelievers will be cast into the lake of fire, where they will remain until the end of the Millennium, when they will be brought out to face Christ a final time for eternal sentencing at the Great White Throne Judgment (Revelation 20:11–15).

Many have wondered why Christ implied that good deeds will be the basis upon which He will determine each person's salvation at the Judgment of the Gentiles, rather than saving faith (Matthew 25:35–36). The answer is that true salvation is evidenced by the fruit of good works, as pointed out in James 2:14–26. John MacArthur explains this, saying, "The deeds are not the basis for their entrance into the kingdom, but merely manifestations of God's grace in their lives. They are the objective criteria for judgment, because they are the evidence of saving faith."[21]

Groundbreaking for the Millennial Temple

Amillennialists, postmillennialists, and premillennialists vigorously debate whether or not there will be a temple in Jerusalem during the Millennium, and if such a temple will exist, why animal sacrifices will be offered at it. In chapter 6, we will give consideration to the biblical evidence for and against such a temple, but I am convinced that a temple will indeed be constructed for use in Christ's earthly kingdom. (This temple should not be confused with the "Tribulation temple" that will also be built prior to the Millennium, and possibly even before the Rapture occurs.) Premillennialists generally agree that Christ's throne will be set up in a magnificent temple located in Jerusalem and that this temple is described in Ezekiel 40–48. Often referred to as "Ezekiel's Temple," it will be much larger and more ornate than the temple used during the Tribulation.

Some believe the Tribulation temple and millennial temple are one in the same, but several facts make it clear they are distinct from each other. Zechariah reveals the Messiah will personally oversee the temple's construction (Zechariah 6:9–15), and this obviously cannot be the Tribulation temple, since Christ will not return to the earth until the end of the Tribulation. Also, Ezekiel's Temple design differs dramatically from the temple plan given in the Law of Moses that we might assume would be used by modern Israel as a template for designing the Tribulation temple. Furthermore, Ezekiel's Temple will contain no wall of partition to exclude Gentiles and no Court of the Women, and this accords with Isaiah 2:2–3 that indicates Gentiles will participate alongside Jews in worship at the millennial temple.

These reasons conclusively show that the millennial temple is not the temple that will exist during the Tribulation and that it will not be constructed until after Christ returns to earth. This temple may not be completed prior to the launch of the Millennium, but it is reasonable to assume construction will begin during the forty-five-day interregnum.

Tribulation Cleanup

Considering the planet-wide devastation that will occur during the last three and a half years of the Tribulation, putting the world back in order to make it habitable by human beings once again will require enormous effort by governments, hired laborers, and the general populace. At least one half of the world's population will have been killed, and cities around the globe will have been reduced to rubble by the various judgments in the Book of Revelation and by earthquakes and other natural disasters. Scripture indicates this massive work of restoration will extend into the Millennium.

In Ezekiel 39, Scripture provides a glimpse of the cleanup process as it will take place in Israel, where Christ will have destroyed the armies gathered against Him at Armageddon. So many corpses of the defeated armies will litter the countryside that mass burials will continue for seven months. A massive graveyard will be established for this purpose in a valley east of the Dead Sea in present-day Jordan. Graves will be so numerous and the burial site so enormous that travel in the area will have to be rerouted. The burial area will be called the Valley of Hamon Gog, or "The Valley of the Hordes of Gog," and will serve as a sobering reminder of God's awesome power (Ezekiel 39:11).

Even after seven months of burials, many human remains will have been overlooked in the initial searches, and they will have decomposed, leaving only scattered bones. Teams of searchers will fan out in a final cleanup sweep to comb the land for remains, and whenever a human bone is found, a marker will be placed beside it. "I've got one over here!" a searcher may call out. "Two more here!" another may shout. Crews will come behind the searchers and collect the remains for burial in the Valley of Hamon Gog (Ezekiel 39:15). This grim task will involve so many workers that an entire town—perhaps a tent city—will spring up as a base of operations, and it will be called Hamonah, a form of the Hebrew word for "hordes" (Ezekiel 39:16). These efforts by the Jewish workers will probably not be motivated by a desire to give their enemies a decent burial as much as by the need to cleanse the land of what defiles it.

Another chore associated with the post-Armageddon cleanup operations will involve disposing of countless armaments that will be found scattered throughout Israel. For seven full years, the people will gather up these implements of warfare and use what parts of them they can for fuel (Ezekiel 39:9).

Cleanups following military conflicts have been necessary wherever warfare has occurred. Following World War II, years were spent cleaning up and rebuilding the ruined cities of Europe. To this day, parts of Germany remain scattered with thousands of tons of unexploded ordnance from the Nazi era. Of course, the Armageddon campaign will leave even worse desolation. In the early years of the Millennium, the rusting relics of war will remind those who gather them up of the miraculous victory won by their God-King. "From that day forward the house of Israel will know that I am the Lord their God" (Ezekiel 39:22).

In addition to these four events that are mentioned in Scripture that will occur following Christ's return, other preparations for the millennial kingdom will presumably take place, including the establishment of Christ's millennial government. Then, when everything has been made ready, the kingdom will commence with a fabulous inaugural event that the Bible calls the marriage supper of the Lamb.

Marriage Supper of the Lamb

At some point after Christ's Second Coming, history's most anticipated celebration will take place. It will happen on earth, and some interpreters believe it will last for the entire one thousand years of Christ's reign! In Revelation 19:6–10, John the apostle is given a preview of the Supper, and he describes hearing the thunderous roar of a vast multitude of believers in heaven who shout, "Hallelujah, for our Lord God Almighty reigns. Let us rejoice and be glad and give him glory!" (vv. 6–7). John is so overcome by what he sees and hears that he falls to the ground in spontaneous worship.

The significance of the Marriage Supper of the Lamb was foreshadowed in Jewish marriage customs that were observed in Jesus's day. Marriage in ancient Israel involved three phases. First came the betrothal, in which the couple's parents met together and formally arranged the marriage. This phase sometimes took place when the bride and groom were still children. Then, nearer to the time for the wedding, came the presentation that included several days of festivities in which the bride and groom's entire family participated. Finally, the formal marriage ceremony took place in which vows were exchanged and the couple became husband and wife. Each of these phases symbolizes an important aspect of Christ's relationship with the believers.

Throughout the New Testament, the church is pictured as the Bride of Christ (2 Corinthians 11:2; Ephesians 5:25–27; Revelation 19:7–9). God "betrothed" the church to Christ in eternity past, and at the Rapture, the church will be presented to Him (John 14:1–3). As with ancient Hebrew marriage suppers, the Marriage Supper of the Lamb will be a time of rejoicing. It will take the form of a magnificent feast attended by Christ Himself and by all believers who will have lived throughout history.

At the Last Supper, Jesus transformed the Passover meal of the Jews into a timeless reminder of His crucifixion. Christians refer to this observance as the Lord's Supper, Communion, or the Eucharist. At the Last Supper, Jesus looked ahead to the Marriage Supper of the Lamb when He told His disciples, "I tell you, I will not drink of this fruit of the vine from now on until that day when I drink it anew with you in my Father's kingdom" (Matthew 26:29). This statement by Christ not only pinpoints the Millennium as the time and place for the Marriage Supper, but it also adds another dimension of meaning to Lord's Supper that we celebrate today. When we observe the Lord's Supper, we are not only looking backward to Christ's sacrificial death on the cross, but we are also looking forward to His earthly kingdom that will be inaugurated with an observance of the same meal by Him and His people in that glorious age to come.

Residents of the Millennium

One of the most striking aspects of life on earth during the Millennium is the wide assortment of people groups living in it, including mortal human beings and immortals in their glorified bodies. Three distinct people groups will populate the millennial kingdom: 1) mortals who survive the Tribulation or are born during the Millennium and who are converted to Christ; 2) mortals born during the Millennium who reject Christ and remain unsaved; and 3) Old Testament saints and believers in Christ who will have died and who return with Christ in their immortal bodies at the Second Coming. When we factor the various ethnicities and age groups into this mixture, we discover millennial society will be the most diverse society in history.

Some of the mortal human beings who live in the millennial kingdom will be Gentiles who will have survived the Tribulation. These are the "sheep" of the Judgment of the Gentiles we discussed earlier in this chapter. Other mortals will be Jewish believers who were converted to Christ during the Tribulation and who live to enter the kingdom, and finally, Jews and Gentiles who are born during the Millennium and who put faith in Christ for salvation. All of these mortals will possess the same abilities and limitations as humans on earth do today, including a sin nature, a personal need for salvation, the ability to produce children, and susceptibility to physical death. Their shared subjection to Christ as their Messiah-King will unite them as one people.

At the Millennium's outset, no unbelievers will be present on earth, because all unsaved persons will have either died during the Tribulation or been removed by Christ at the Judgment of the Gentiles or the judgment of Israel. Every person in the kingdom will be a regenerate child of God. However, this initial spiritual equality will not last, because children born to mortals during the Millennium will need to believe on Christ for salvation, just as people do today, but many of them will not do so, and they will multiply into an ever-increasing population of unbelievers throughout the thousand years. Then, when Satan is released from the Abyss near the end of the Millennium, he will incite these unredeemed ones to rebel against Christ and attempt to overthrow Him.

As mentioned already, mortal humans living in the Millennium will be subject to physical death, and many Bible students have wondered what will happen to those who do. Unsaved humans who die in the Millennium will be resurrected at the end of the Millennium along with unbelievers who die prior to it, and all will be sentenced by Christ to the lake of fire at the Great White Throne Judgment. As for born-again mortals who die during the Millennium, Scripture contains no information about their resurrection. God will either raise them instantly to live on earth for the remainder of the thousand years as immortals, or resurrect them at the end of the Millennium. Whatever the case, we can be certain they will live eternally with God.

As we consider all these events destined to take place in preparation for the Millennium, the sheer scope of transformation that Christ's earthly kingdom will bring to our planet astounds us. At the dawn of the Millennium, the earth will have been rescued from oblivion, and Satan will have been removed and locked away. Righteousness and peace will bless humankind, and God's people from every period of history will live together on earth in a world presided over by Christ Himself.

What a mind-blowing future lies ahead for God's people! No wonder the prophetic portions of Scripture focus upon the Millennium more than any other topic. These glimpses of the coming kingdom give us ample cause for rejoicing, and they pique our curiosity and make us eager to know more. Death becomes far less dreadful when we discover how much awaits us in the glorious kingdom Christ will bring to our planet.

3

Life in the New World

Joy to the world, the Lord is come!
Let earth receive her King.

—"Joy to the World," Isaac Watts[22]

Have you ever noticed that many of our most well-known and beloved Christmas songs make reference to the Millennium? It is appropriate they do, because the Bible presents Christ's birth as a precursor to His return and millennial reign. When the angel Gabriel announced to Mary that she would bear the Messiah, he looked far beyond the Messiah's birth to His eternal earthly kingdom when he said, "He will be great and will be called the Son of the Most High. The Lord God will give him the throne of his father David, and he will reign over the house of Jacob forever; his kingdom will never end" (Luke 1:32–33). For centuries, Christian songwriters have recognized this connection and drawn inspiration from portions of Scripture that link Christ's birth to His future kingdom on earth. Here are some familiar examples:

And by the light of that same star
Three wise men came from country far;

To seek for a king was their intent.
—"The First Nowell," Davies Gilbert[23]

Hark! the herald angels sing,
"Glory to the newborn King!"
—"Hark! The Herald Angels Sing,"
Charles Wesley and George Whitefield[24]

Peace on the earth, good will to men,
From heaven's all gracious King!
—"It Came Upon a Midnight
Clear," Edmund H. Sears[25]

The King of Kings lay thus in lowly manger
In all our trials born to be our friend.
—"O Holy Night," Placide
Cappeau and Adolphe C. Adam[26]

Born a King on Bethlehem's plain
Gold I bring to crown Him again
King forever, ceasing never
Over us all to reign.
—"We Three Kings of Orient
Are," John H. Hopkins[27]

Probably the most famous example of Christmas music that anticipates Christ's millennial kingdom is the triumphal movement from Handel's *Messiah*, which is a verbatim quote of Isaiah 9:5–6 set to music:

Every warrior's boot used in battle and every garment rolled in blood will be destined for burning, will be fuel for the fire. For to us a child is born, to us a son is given, and the government will be on his shoulders. And he will be called Wonderful Counselor, Mighty God, Everlasting Father, Prince of Peace.[28]

Similarly, the nineteenth-century Scottish poet James Montgomery looked beyond Christ's birth to His future reign when he penned these lyrics of the hymn, "Angels from the Realms of Glory," so often sung at Christmastime:

> Though an infant now we view him,
> He shall fill his Father's throne,
> Gather all the nations to him;
> Every knee shall then bow down.[29]

These and similar Christmas songs highlight the connection made again and again in Scripture between Christ's first coming and His eventual return. Jesus will indeed rule the world someday as King of kings and Lord of lords. His kingdom will encompass the entire planet, and all nations will bow to His authority, "And Christ will have the prize for which He died—An inheritance of nations."[30]

If you are a born-again believer, when the Millennium begins, you will either have died and been taken to heaven or will have been caught up to meet Christ at the Rapture of the church. You will return with Christ to earth in your glorified body that is free of your old sin nature and the limitations of the flesh. Your mind will have been enlightened by God and enabled to fully comprehend His mysteries and understand His purposes and His ways. Paul assures us of this transformation of believers by saying, "Now we see but a poor reflection as in a mirror; then we shall see face to face. Now I know in part; then I shall know fully, even as I am fully known" (1 Corinthians 13:12).

As an immortal child of God, you will never again experience anxiety, fear, insecurity, loneliness, or any other negative emotion, and you will instead know absolute peace and contentment. As humanity on earth suffered unspeakable anguish during the Great Tribulation, you will have lived in the glorious presence of Christ and God in heaven.

Back to Earth

At the Second Coming, you will return with Christ to a shattered earth—desolated by the apocalyptic judgments of the Great Tribulation. Human survivors who have put their faith in Christ during the Tribulation will welcome the Messiah's return with shouts of praise and celebration, but unbelievers will retreat in terror from the Lord whom they have willfully rejected. The entire planet will lie in ruins—an astounding panorama of death and destruction caused by unspeakable calamities. Whole continents will have been decimated, and once-beautiful landscapes will have become scorched wastelands.

Nonetheless, these sights will not depress you because you will know that "the great day of God Almighty" (Revelation 16:14) is over and that Christ has reclaimed the earth for Himself. Perhaps you will feel wave of revulsion as you view the result of years of Satan's domination, but you will rejoice in knowing that the forces of evil are expelled and the dawn of Christ's earthly kingdom has come.

Features of the New World

In this chapter, we will explore descriptions of the new world that God has implanted in Scripture. Although details about the Millennium are scattered throughout the Bible like pieces of a jigsaw puzzle, we will carefully fit them together so that they form a thrilling and beautiful picture. Scripture unveils many features of the Millennium that, when seen together, help us see how truly glorious it will be.

Satan Gone

Save for the presence of Christ, the absence of Satan will contribute to the glory of the Millennium more than any other aspect of it. Imagine the thrill you and other resurrected believers will experience as you return from heaven to live in a world with no devil in it! The serpent will have been cast out of Eden, and for one thousand years, humankind on earth will enjoy complete freedom from the devil's oppression and evil schemes.

Society Permeated by Righteousness

Satan's imprisonment will result in a dramatic lessening of sin committed by mortal humans living on earth. Nevertheless, although Satan will not be present during most of the Millennium to entice them to do evil, every mortal—including ones who are converted to Christ—will still possess a sin nature that predisposes them to rebel against God, just as mortals possess today. Thankfully, all mortal human beings who enter His kingdom at its beginning will be born again, and the Holy Spirit will reside within them and curb their inclination to sin. As the prophet Isaiah declared, "the earth will be full of the knowledge of the LORD as the waters cover the sea" (Isaiah 11:9; cf. Jeremiah 31:34).

Isaiah describes how this knowledge of God will manifest itself particularly within the nation of Israel. Speaking of Israelites who will live in the millennial kingdom, he says, "Then the eyes of those who see will no longer be closed, and the ears of those who hear will listen" (Isaiah 32:3). God will bless born-again Jews with extraordinary spiritual perception and insight, and so Israel will serve as a model of godliness for all other nations and will epitomize theocratic government under the headship of Christ.

Addressing societal values in the future kingdom, Isaiah adds, "No longer will the fool be called noble nor the scoundrel be highly respected" (Isaiah 32:5). Godless and profane persons will no longer be idolized or emulated as they are so often today.

Partial Phaseout of the Curse

When most Christians envision the Millennium, they anticipate an entire planet transformed into a paradise, with all the millennial blessings described in Scripture applying equally to every part of the globe. For many years, I too understood the Scriptures to predict that the entire natural world will be perfected when Christ returns, but as I investigated what the Bible actually says about these transformations foretold in Scripture, I became convinced that the curse will be lifted only partially during the Millennium and that most of the Eden-like conditions in the natural world will exist only in Israel.

When Adam and Eve disobeyed God by eating from the Tree of the Knowledge of Good and Evil, their sin brought disastrous consequences to themselves, the natural world, and every living thing in it, including their expulsion from the Garden of Eden and God's pronouncement of a curse upon "the ground." God said to Adam:

> "Because you listened to your wife and ate from the tree about which I commanded you, 'You must not eat of it,' Cursed is the ground because of you; through painful toil you will eat of it all the days of your life. It will produce thorns and thistles for you, and you will eat the plants of the field. By the sweat of your brow you will eat your food until you return to the ground, since from it you were taken; for dust you are and to dust you will return." (Genesis 3:17–19)

The apostle Paul makes it clear the curse God pronounced extended to the entire physical universe:

> The creation waits in eager expectation for the sons of God to be revealed. For the creation was subjected to frustration, not by its own choice, but by the will of the one who subjected it, in hope that the creation itself will be liberated from its bondage to decay and brought into the glorious freedom of the children of God. We know that *the whole creation has been groaning as in the pains of childbirth right up to the present time.* (Romans 8:19–22)

In the years following Adam and Eve's banishment from the Garden of Eden, the effects of God's curse upon the natural world became ever more evident. Sickness and disease, famine and death began to take their toll upon human beings. Carnage pervaded the animal world as creatures began to prey upon one another for food, and natural disasters, including earthquakes, volcanoes, droughts, and destructive storms, became common occurrences. Then, following the Great Flood recorded in Genesis, human life spans were shortened dramatically. Because of the curse, we live in a world in which things fall apart and physical, social, and personal disintegration are the norm.

The Bible declares that, in the Millennium, God will begin to lift His curse upon the natural world, but He will eliminate it in two successive stages, rather than all at once. The first stage will take place during the Millennium, and the second stage in the eternal state that follows it. In the Millennium, God will lift elements of the curse only in the land of Israel, and in the eternal state, He will lift the curse entirely from the whole earth,[31] and thus the apostle John declares in Revelation 22:3 that, once the eternal state arrives, "No longer will there be any curse." All traces of sin and its consequences will be removed forever.

Let's return for a moment to those Millennium-focused Christmas songs we mentioned earlier. Some of the songs, including Isaac Watts's beloved "Joy to the World," which he based upon Psalm 98, assume that God will eliminate the curse throughout the world in the Millennium:

> No more let sins and sorrows grow,
> Nor thorns infest the ground;
> He comes to make His blessings flow
> Far as the curse is found,
> Far as the curse is found,
> Far as, far as, the curse is found.[32]

Watts's lyrics reflect the general assumption that idyllic conditions in the Millennium, including abundant food harvests, human longevity, and the disappearance of predation in the animal kingdom, will exist everywhere on earth. However, as I have stated, I am convinced that a careful reading of Scripture reveals most such predictions apply exclusively to Palestine. Even the great nineteenth-century Millennium expert Nathaniel West stopped short of declaring that the Millennium will witness a total rollback of the curse, saying rather, "To what extent the glorification of our planet shall go, at the Second Coming of the Son of Man, is a point left undetermined in the Scriptures."[33] It becomes easier to recognize this truth when we remember that one of God's primary purposes for the Millennium is to glorify Israel in the eyes of the nations.

As we saw in chapter 1, in the Millennium God will fulfill all of His covenantal promises to Abraham and his descendants. As John MacArthur notes, "The streams of the Abrahamic, Davidic, and New Covenants find their confluence in the millennial kingdom ruled over by the Messiah."[34] Premillennialists typically refer to the Millennium as "the time of Israel's glory." It therefore follows that Israel will enjoy particular blessings during the Millennium that other nations will not.

We must also be careful not to conflate Christ's worldwide rule and His elimination of the curse but to keep them separate, because failure to recognize their distinctiveness from each other leads to great confusion. Because Christ's kingdom will encompass the entire earth, many students of prophecy assume that all the millennial blessings foretold in Scripture will extend globally as well, but this interpretive leap is unsupported by Scripture. In reality, Scripture makes it clear that, although Christ will reign over all nations, He will reserve His greatest blessings for His covenant people.

Isaiah declares this clearly, pointing out that the land of Israel will flourish agriculturally and provide abundant food for the world: "In days to come Jacob will take root, Israel will bud and blossom and fill all the world with fruit" (Isaiah 27:6).

Similarly, Ezekiel 36:33–36 indicates God's promise of millennial restoration applies exclusively to the land of Israel:

> "This is what the Sovereign LORD says: On the day I cleanse you from all your sins, I will resettle your towns, and the ruins will be rebuilt. The desolate land will be cultivated instead of lying desolate in the sight of all who pass through it. They will say, '*This land that was laid waste has become like the Garden of Eden*; the cities that were lying in ruins, desolate and destroyed, are now fortified and inhabited.' Then the nations around you that remain will know that I the LORD have rebuilt what was destroyed and have replanted what was desolate. I the LORD have spoken, and I will do it."

Notice God does not promise restoration of all land on earth, but only of *this* land.

Further evidence that utopian conditions will exist only in the land of Israel during the Millennium is seen in prophecies of the Messiah's stern dealings with nations that disobey Him when He reigns on earth. Psalm 2:9 declares that the Messiah "will rule them with an iron scepter; [and] will dash them to pieces like pottery." Zechariah 14:17 foretells that if nations refuse to join in the celebration of the Feast of Tabernacles during the Millennium, they will suffer punitive droughts, but if the curse is repealed in those nations, how could droughts occur in them?

A Stunning Makeover

Some blessings of the Millennium will certainly be enjoyed by everyone on earth, wherever they may live. Scripture indicates astrophysical changes will enhance the quality life for people in every part of the globe. Isaiah 30:26 says "The moon will shine like the sun, and the sunlight will be seven times brighter, like the light of seven full days, when the LORD binds up the bruises of his people and heals the wounds he inflicted." Although this prophecy primarily pertained to ancient Judah, many Bible interpreters believe Isaiah's prediction will find its ultimate fulfillment in the millennial reign of Christ when God blesses the Jewish people with a time of abundance.

We must acknowledge that serious scientific problems come with taking Isaiah's prediction of a sevenfold increase in the sun's light literally. Such an occurrence would, under normal circumstances, cook our planet and render it inhospitable to most life forms! On the other hand, who knows how God might adjust the laws of nature to accommodate such transformations? As Old Testament scholars Keil and Delitzsch explain,

> No other miracles will be needed for this than that wonder-working power of God, which will then give the greatest brilliancy and most unchangeable duration to … a perfectly unclouded sky, with sun or moon shining in all its brilliancy, yet without any

> scorching from the one, or injurious effects from the other.[35]

Israel Glorified

God will bring amazing transformations to the Holy Land during the Millennium that will cause Israel to become the envy of the entire world. One such blessing will be runaway food production, for Ezekiel 34:29 says that Israel will become a breadbasket during the Millennium as God makes Palestine "a land renowned for its crops." God will cause Israel's farmland to produce harvests of unbelievable abundance, and crop yields will increase dramatically and with far less effort required for cultivation. "'The days are coming,' declares the LORD, 'when the reaper will be overtaken by the plowman and the planter by the one treading grapes. New wine will drip from the mountains and flow from all the hills'" (Amos 9:13). Crops will grow so rapidly that planting and harvest seasons will overlap each other! This may indicate a modification of Israel's climate, resulting in year-round growing seasons.

God specified that He will bestow these agricultural blessings exclusively upon Israel in the Millennium, saying, "'The seed will grow well, the vine will yield its fruit, the ground will produce its crops, and the heavens will drop their dew. I will give all these things as an inheritance *to the remnant of this people*'" (Zechariah 8:12). "This people" refers to the people of Israel.

Dry and barren regions of Israel, such as the Negev that lies south of Jerusalem, will become garden spots, well watered and lush with vegetation (Isaiah 35:1–2, 7; 51:3; Ezekiel 34:26–27, 29; 36:35; Joel 3:18; Zechariah 8:12). Israel's agricultural abundance will showcase to the world God's favor and blessing upon His chosen people and will symbolize the Holy Spirit's powerful presence with them: "'For I will pour water on the thirsty land, and streams on the dry ground; I will pour out my Spirit on your offspring, and my blessing on your descendants'" (Isaiah 44:3). As surely as regular rains will saturate Israel's desert lands with life-giving water, the Holy Spirit will inhabit the Jewish people and bless them with righteousness.

Plentiful harvests in Israel during the Millennium may result to some degree from agricultural expertise provided by God. Historians Will and Ariel Durant have claimed that, "if current agricultural knowledge were everywhere applied, the planet could feed twice its present population."[36] Given this fact, imagine what abundance God-given farming skills, coupled with ideal weather conditions, will produce! As Israel's farmers produce plentiful food, famine and hunger will disappear in Palestine.

The Bible also foretells an end to predatory behavior among animals in Israel during the Millennium, and the image of a lion lying peacefully alongside a lamb has become the most widely recognized symbol of the eschaton. Animals that now prey upon one another will coexist without aggression in Israel—as they did prior to Adam and Eve's sin and expulsion from the Garden of Eden. Imagine dangerous carnivores suddenly becoming harmless plant eaters:

> The wolf will live with the lamb, the leopard will lie down with the goat, the calf and the lion and the yearling together; and a little child will lead them. (Isaiah 11:6)

> "'The lion will eat straw like the ox, but dust will be the serpent's food. They will neither harm nor destroy on all my holy mountain,' says the LORD." (Isaiah 65:25)

God's "holy mountain" refers to the city of Jerusalem and the Temple Mount, as it frequently does elsewhere in the Old Testament (Psalm 48:1; Isaiah 27:13; 56:7; 66:20; Zechariah 8:3), indicating this blessing may be restricted to that vicinity or to the region of Palestine.

The reason this transformation of predatory animals will occur in Israel only and not throughout the world is given in Ezekiel 34:25–32 and Hosea 2:18–23, where God promises a future "covenant of peace" He will make with Israel. Both prophets mention that this covenant will include peace with wild animals, so the people of Israel can live safely in their ancestral land. Isaiah 11:8 says, "The infant will play near the hole of the cobra, and the young child put his hand into the viper's nest." Cobras are ranked among the world's most venomous snakes, yet during the Millennium, toddlers in Israel will play near their dens in absolute safety.

One observer notes, "Nature provides for almost all of our needs and it is as diverse as the stars in the sky. But there is a dark side too. Nature also contains some of the most awful things you can imagine—worse than anything conjured up by Stephen King!"[37] It therefore seems likely that the elimination of predatory behavior will extend to every level of the zoological order within Israel, including mammals, reptiles, sea creatures, and even insects. God's taming of wild beasts in Israel will display the grace He lavishes upon His covenant people, and it will astound the world.

In our scientific age, the idea of carnivores instantly becoming herbivores seems like the stuff of fairy tales, and liberal interpreters dismiss the literal fulfillment of these prophecies. However, faith does not require us to explain the physiological changes involved in meat eaters becoming plant eaters, any more than we must explain how Jesus transformed water into wine or how God physically raises dead people to life. As with all of the Bible's claims involving the miraculous, we must simply take our omnipotent God at His word. I am astounded that God created the very first lion out of nothing, and so I have no difficulty believing He will someday make a lion that eats straw!

A New Ethic for Business and Commerce

Everyday life will continue in the future messianic kingdom that you will inhabit. Farmers will grow crops and raise livestock, factories will produce goods, banks will manage deposits and invest capital, schools will educate students, and governments will pass laws and administer state affairs. The great difference in the Millennium will be that all such activities will take place free of Satan's corrupting influence and under Christ's astute supervision. This will lead to dramatic reductions in evils such as political corruption, crime, domestic conflict, immorality, and hedonistic self-indulgence. In your glorified body, you will be immune to all such vices, and mortal humans living around you, although still subject to their allure, will find them less enticing.

Today, criminal activity inflicts the people of the world with enormous unnecessary suffering. In a report the federal government published more than a hundred years ago, Eugene Smith wrote, "The mental suffering and agony, the ruined lives, the broken homes and hearts, the desolation and yearning and despair—who can measure the cost of crime?"[38] In 2013, the United Nations Office of Drugs and Crime put the global cost of crime at $2.1 trillion.[39] One estimate put the total monetary cost of crime in the United States alone at $1.7 trillion per year, including expenses borne by the legal system, the cost of anticrime measures, crime-related injuries and deaths, and lost productivity.[40] According to a report published by researchers at Iowa State University, every burglary in the US costs over $41,000, and every murder costs over $17 million in investigation, prosecution, and long-term incarceration costs. Based upon that estimate, serial killer Gary Ridgway, the infamous Green River Killer, cost the United States $216 million.[41]

In the Millennium, crime will be drastically reduced in all nations, particularly in the early years when most of the world's citizens will put faith in Christ. In Isaiah 32:18, God promises the people of Israel, "'My people will live in peaceful dwelling places, in secure homes, in undisturbed places of rest.'" Scripture's numerous references to worldwide peace and safety indicate this blessing will extend to all nations and not to Israel only.

Throughout the Millennium, Christ's government will deal swiftly and severely with every hostile act on the part of the nations. Psalm 2:9 says of Israel's Messiah, "'You will rule them with an iron scepter; you will dash them to pieces like pottery.'" Similarly, Isaiah 11:4 declares, "He will strike the earth with the rod of his mouth; with the breath of his lips he will slay the wicked." Christ will judge all wrongdoing during the Millennium and thus will maintain a global society in which criminal activity is held in check.

Christ's curtailing of crime during the Millennium will bring dramatic improvements to the quality of everyday life, chiefly in Israel, and to some extent throughout the world. Vast resources needed now for law enforcement, criminal justice, and crime prevention will be freed up for more productive uses. No longer will every door need to be locked at night and all possessions secured from theft or vandalism. As a result, the market for products that are must-haves today like security lighting, security systems, and surveillance cameras will drop, and people will walk city streets at night in safety.

As crime diminishes and freedom from want and fear flourishes, human creativity and productivity will experience a renaissance as people are set free from such concerns to enjoy the fruits of their labors. Psalm 72:7 says of the Messiah's earthly reign, "In his days the righteous will flourish; prosperity will abound till the moon is no more." Life for Christ's faithful followers will become truly abundant and satisfying, as God made it to be prior to sin's entrance into the world.

Peace, Not War

James Madison wrote, "Of all the enemies to public liberty, war is, perhaps, the most to be dreaded because it comprises and develops the germ of every other."[42] Throughout history, hostilities between nations have taken a devastating toll upon the human race. The *New York Times* reported in 2003 that only 268 years of the past 3,400 years of recorded human history have been entirely free of military conflict, meaning more than 90 percent of recorded history has been marked by warfare. The article went on to report that no less than 108 million people died in wars during the twentieth century alone, and the total number of war-related fatalities throughout all of human history could be as high as one billion.[43]

Today, the world's combined armed forces total more than twenty-one million people.[44] World military spending hovers at around $2.5 trillion each year, or approximately 2.5 percent of the entire world's annual gross domestic product. That equates to about $250 per year for every man, woman, and child on earth.[45] Coupled with the inestimable toll of warfare in terms of human suffering, destroyed infrastructure, economic impact, harm to the environment, and other losses, warfare is by far the costliest to the human race.

It is therefore impossible to quantify the positive impact of war's end to life on earth during the Millennium. George Washington's favorite Bible verse was Micah 4:4, which happens to be a millennial prophecy: "Every man will sit under his own vine and under his own fig tree, and no one will make them afraid, for the LORD Almighty has spoken." In that verse, Micah envisions the peace and prosperity that will be enjoyed by Israel and the entire world in the Millennium. In a letter Washington wrote in August 1790 to a Jewish congregation in Newport, Rhode Island, he said, "May the children of the stock of Abraham who dwell in this land continue to merit and enjoy the good will of the other inhabitants—while every one shall sit in safety under his own vine and fig tree and there shall be none to make him afraid."[50]

Isaiah 2:4 foretells that, when Christ reigns on earth, "He will judge between the nations and will settle disputes for many peoples. They will beat their swords into plowshares and their spears into pruning hooks. Nation will not take up sword against nation, nor will they train for war anymore." Elsewhere, God Himself declares, "'Bow and sword and battle I will abolish from the land, so that all may lie down in safety'" (Hosea 2:18). International peace will rank among the paramount blessings enjoyed by the citizens of Christ's earthly kingdom, and the angels' declaration of "'on earth peace to men on whom his favor rests'" made to the shepherds on the night of Christ's birth (Luke 2:14) will at last find its fulfillment.

Warfare's termination will make it possible for the entire $2.5 trillion in worldwide annual military-related spending to be saved, or redirected toward nobler purposes, year after year, and over the entire course of the Millennium. Altogether, the savings could equal at least $1 *quadrillion*, or $\$10^{15}$ trillion, which, when written out, is 10 followed by fifteen zeroes! We cannot imagine the mind-boggling benefits for humanity that will result from such a reallocation of financial resources!

Human Life Spans in Israel Greatly Extended

More than three thousand years ago, Moses declared, "The length of our days is seventy years—or eighty, if we have the strength" (Psalm 90:10). According to the World Health Organization, the average human life span today remains relatively unchanged at seventy-one years worldwide.[46] In the Millennium, however, life expectancy for the people of Israel will increase dramatically, as foretold by the prophet Isaiah:

> "But be glad and rejoice forever in what I will create, for I will create Jerusalem to be a delight and its people a joy. I will rejoice over Jerusalem and take delight in my people; the sound of weeping and of crying will be heard in it no more. Never again will there be in it an infant who lives but a few days, or an old man who does not live out his years; he who dies at a hundred will be thought a mere youth; he who fails to reach a hundred will be considered accursed. They will build houses and dwell in them; they will plant vineyards and eat their fruit. No longer will they build houses and others live in them, or plant and others eat. For as the days of a tree, so will be the days of my people; my chosen ones will long enjoy the works of their hands." (Isaiah 65:18–22)

Evidently, God made those promises exclusively to Jews in the Millennium, for the purpose of showcasing His love and favor toward that nation, "'for they will be a people blessed by the LORD, they and their descendants with them'" (Isaiah 65:23). While many Bible interpreters have understood Isaiah's prophecy to apply to all humans alive during the Millennium, Isaiah's repeated references to "Jerusalem" and "its people" make it apparent that it pertains specifically to the people of millennial Israel.

Isaiah declares that infant mortality in Israel will disappear entirely during the Millennium. Furthermore, he says that, in the Millennium, Jews will live so long that any Israeli who dies under the age of a hundred will be presumed to have suffered divine discipline because of personal sin (Isaiah 65:20)! In verse 22 of that chapter, he says average human life expectancy in Israel during the Millennium will be equal to that of trees! Olive trees are among the most common trees in Palestine, and they have a life expectancy of five hundred years. Even if we assume the use of hyperbole by Isaiah, his point still stands: the people of Israel will enjoy extraordinarily long life spans in the Millennium.

Scientists and medical doctors today have not reached a consensus on what causes humans and animals to age and die. Some claim human DNA is preprogrammed to cause our bodies to deteriorate and die, while others believe accumulated cellular damage eventually shuts down our bodies' ability to renew themselves. Any attempt to explain how Jewish life spans will be lengthened during the Millennium would be entirely speculative, and so we will not venture a hypothesis. Whatever means God will use to extend the life spans of Israelites, we know He will do it so that His "chosen ones will long enjoy the works of their hands" (Isaiah 65:22). God will enable His covenant people to enjoy their accomplishments and the fruits of their labors to the very fullest extent possible.

Israelis' physical health will also become more vigorous in the eschaton. "No one living in Zion [Israel] will say, 'I am ill'; and the sins of those who dwell there will be forgiven" (Isaiah 33:24). Disabilities such as blindness, deafness, and inability to walk will vanish altogether in the Holy Land (Isaiah 29:18; 35:5–6). Although Israel today is a leading innovator in the field of health care, few medical doctors will be needed there during the Millennium!

Tares among the Wheat

One of Scripture's least known teachings concerning the Millennium is the fact that unsaved people will live in it. At the beginning of the Millennium, no unredeemed mortals will exist anyplace on earth because, as we saw in chapter 2, at the judgment of the nations just prior to the kingdom, Christ will separate true believers from unbelievers among the Gentiles, and unbelievers will be led away to eternal damnation, but all true believers will be ushered into Christ's kingdom (Matthew 25:31–46). Likewise, at the judgment of Israel, unbelieving Jews will be ferreted out and sent to hell, while redeemed Jews will enter the kingdom. These initial kingdom residents will bear children who need to be redeemed through faith in Christ, just as people do today. Many of them will believe in Christ—probably in far greater numbers than people do in the present age—but not all, and those who reject Christ will remain unsaved.

One indication of unbelievers' presence in the kingdom can be seen in the severity with which the Bible says the Messiah will subjugate "the nations" and rule over them.

> "Ask of me, and I will make the nations your inheritance, the ends of the earth your possession. You will rule them with an iron scepter; you will dash them to pieces like pottery." (Psalm 2:8–9)

> "No enemy will subject him to tribute; no wicked man will oppress him. I will crush his foes before him and strike down his adversaries." (Psalm 89:22–23)

> She [a figurative woman representing the nation of Israel] gave birth to a son, a male child, who will rule all the nations with an iron scepter. (Revelation 12:5)

Obviously, the subjects of these verses cannot be *believers*, because Scripture never calls true believers "wicked" or enemies of Christ, and God's redeemed ones will not require such heavy-handed rule. Such passages in Scripture can only refer to unredeemed humans born during Christ's millennial reign.

Still another clue that unbelievers will live in the Millennium is the retribution Christ will exact upon nations that fail to participate in mandatory worship events during the Millennium. Zechariah the prophet reveals that Christ will require nations of the world to send delegations to Jerusalem to participate annually in the Feast of Tabernacles, and those nations who do not will be disciplined with drought and plagues:

> Then the survivors from all the nations that have attacked Jerusalem will go up year after year to worship the King, the LORD Almighty, and to celebrate the Feast of Tabernacles. If any of the peoples of the earth do not go up to Jerusalem to worship the King, the LORD Almighty, they will have no rain. If the Egyptian people do not go up and take part, they will have no rain. The LORD will bring on them the plague he inflicts on the nations that do not go up to celebrate the Feast of Tabernacles. This will be the punishment of Egypt and the punishment of all the nations that do not go up to celebrate the Feast of Tabernacles. (Zechariah 14:16–19)

When Satan is released from his prison at the end of the Millennium, he will incite many to rebel against Christ (Revelation 20:7–10). Hordes of deceived human beings will surround Jerusalem to attack the Lord and overthrow His government, but before they can launch their assault, Christ will destroy them with fire from heaven. Obviously, true believers could not be persuaded to participate in an attempted coup against the Messiah!

Although realizing that unbelievers will live on earth during the Millennium may surprise and dismay us, the fact that they will provides an important insight into one of the Millennium's purposes in God's end-time program. Their presence demonstrates that the earth will still not be entirely free from the presence of sin. This reality, combined with the fact that human beings will still experience physical death during the Millennium, makes it clear that the Millennium will serve as a parenthesis between this present world and the new earth that will be created after it.

As our sketch of Christ's millennial kingdom takes shape, an incredibly exciting picture emerges of the world you will live in as a resurrected believer. Without a doubt, the Millennium will be the most wonderful and glorious time in history in which to live on planet Earth. More than any other feature of the Millennium, Christ's reign over the world as King of kings makes this true. In the next chapter, we will examine what Scripture foretells about Christ's millennial government, by which He will transform politics into a glorious system of good for all humankind.

4

Christ's Government in the Millennium

> The seventh angel sounded his trumpet, and there were loud voices in heaven, which said: "The kingdom of the world has become the kingdom of our Lord and of his Christ, and he will reign for ever and ever."
>
> —Revelation 11:15

Let's face it, most of us have grumbled about politicians at one time or another. Today's headlines regularly feature exposés of elected officials who have abused their offices and failed their constituents. History is littered with leaders who succumbed to pride, greed, and corruption. Trustworthy and effective leaders have been hard to come by in all generations and in all walks of life, including in government, and even the best leaders possess feet of clay and are limited by flaws and deficiencies of one sort or another.

More than two hundred years ago, James Madison wrote, "If angels were to govern men, neither external nor internal controls on government would be necessary."[47] True, but the human race is the only source we can draw our leaders from, and government leaders are no more flawless than their constituents. William Howard Taft, the twenty-seventh president of the United States, said, "We are imperfect. We cannot expect perfect government." Thus, our shortcomings make checks and balances necessary in order to ensure that leaders are kept accountable.

All this gives us good reason to look forward to the Millennium! During that era, Christ will provide absolutely perfect leadership, and His government will be a true theocracy, characterized by steadfast integrity and trustworthiness. Not only will Christ be invulnerable to corruption, but He also will possess infinite ability to govern. He will sit enthroned as the world's first and only infallible political figure—capable and upright to the core.

Not since Israel's earliest years has any government existed on earth in which the head of state was God, Himself. Under the leadership of Moses and Joshua, Israel's seat of government was the Tabernacle, from which God personally directed national affairs through the administration of the priests. After Joshua's death, Israel strayed from allegiance to God and turned to paganism and idolatry, and this led to one of the darkest periods in Israel's history and gave rise to the judges (see Joshua 2:7–24). At that point, theocratic government vanished from the earth, and it will not exist here again until Christ returns to establish His rule as King of kings. But when His kingdom comes, it will be mightier and more glorious than any government the world has ever known.

Let's delve into what the Bible reveals to us about Christ's future millennial government and your role in it as a glorified saint of God.

Christ's Rule over the Earth

No place in Scripture confirms that Christ's millennial rule will be global in scope more plainly than Zechariah 14:9: "The LORD will be king over the whole earth. On that day there will be one LORD, and his name the only name." All political, economic, and religious authority will be consolidated in Christ, and His dominion will extend to every nation and people group on earth.

As we have seen already, at the Millennium's beginning, every person on earth will be a redeemed believer in Christ and will gladly bow to Christ's authority and follow His leadership. David said of Christ, "He will judge the world in righteousness; he will govern the peoples with justice" (Psalm 9:8). Every decree issued by Christ, every law enacted by Him, and every judgment handed down by Him will be absolutely wise and prudent. Imagine a leader who is totally incorruptible and who makes perfect choices all the time!

Isaiah the prophet used three descriptive titles to define the noble character of Christ's rule during the Millennium:

> For to us a child is born, to us a son is given, and the government will be on his shoulders. And he will be called Wonderful Counselor, Mighty God, Everlasting Father, Prince of Peace. (Isaiah 9:6)

Each of these titles represents a particular facet of Christ's leadership as King of kings on earth. As "Wonderful Counselor," Christ will provide divine guidance to the peoples of the earth and will lead with perfect knowledge. As "Mighty God," His authority will be absolute and will extend to every corner of the world. As "Everlasting Father," Christ will be acknowledged as God, and He will care for His people as a father cares for his children, by meeting their needs (Isaiah 40:11) and providing love and discipline (Proverbs 3:12). As "Prince of Peace," He will end all warfare and settle disputes among nations. Elsewhere, Isaiah describes Christ's role as the world's peacemaker:

He will judge between the nations and will settle disputes for many peoples. They will beat their swords into plowshares and their spears into pruning hooks. Nation will not take up sword against nation, nor will they train for war anymore. (Isaiah 2:4)

A Stern Ruler

During the Millennium, God the Father will sovereignly cause all nations to be subjugated under Christ's absolute authority and rule. In Psalm 110:1, David records that the Father declared at some point in the undated past to make His Son the unrivaled sovereign over the earth: "The LORD says to my Lord: 'Sit at my right hand until I make your enemies a footstool for your feet.'" John MacArthur explains the historical background of this imagery:

> At God's right hand, the Messiah would be invincible, because God would put His enemies beneath His feet, a figure of abject, helpless subjugation. When a defeated enemy was brought before an ancient oriental monarch, the ruler would make the prisoner prostate himself at his feet. The king would then place his foot on the neck of the vanquished enemy as if he were a footstool (see Joshua 10:24).[48]

God the Father and Christ will accomplish this progressively over the entire span of the Millennium. Then, at the end of the Millennium, Christ will deal finally and conclusively with all unsaved humans who will have ever lived, and with Satan and the demons, by casting them into in the lake of fire where they will undergo everlasting torment.

Christ's subjugation of all humans living on earth and His judgment of unbelievers and the spiritual forces of evil is vital to grasping the Father's ultimate purpose for Christ's millennial reign. While it is certainly true that God the Father will use the Millennium to bring to fruition all of His covenantal promises to the nation of Israel, God's *primary* objective for the Millennium is the glorification of His Son, which will transpire as Christ defeats every enemy and quells all opposition to Him.

The apostle Paul reveals in 1 Corinthians 15:24–26 that, during the Millennium, Christ's supremacy and dominion will extend over all realms, including the natural and the supernatural:

> Then the end will come, when he hands over the kingdom to God the Father after he has destroyed all dominion, authority and power. For he must reign until he has put all his enemies under his feet. The last enemy to be destroyed is death.

Anthony Thiselton believes "all dominion, authority and power" refers to "any kind of structural opposition to God, whether social, political, economic, ethical, spiritual, or even … 'supernatural.'"[49] Thus we see that Christ will rule with unrivaled power in the Millennium. Zero tolerance will be shown to any nation that resists His authority. Herbert Vander Lugt says the Messiah will "place people under complete restraint so that among the citizens of the kingdom, sin will be rare by today's standards and judgment for wrongdoing will be administered quickly and justly."[50]

In Ecclesiastes 8:11, Solomon observes that, "When the sentence for a crime is not quickly carried out, the hearts of the people are filled with schemes to do wrong." Because this is true, evil often proliferates in our present age, but in the Millennium, Christ will mete out perfect justice and instant punishment upon all who do wrong. People everywhere will live in far greater safety and security in His peaceable kingdom than anyone on earth enjoys now.

Once Christ accomplishes this, Paul's declaration in Philippians 2:10–11 will come to pass:

> At the name of Jesus every knee [will] bow, in heaven and on earth and under the earth, and every tongue confess that Jesus Christ is Lord, to the glory of God the Father. (Philippians 2:10–11)

In 1 Corinthians 15:27b–28, Paul goes on to say:

> Now when it says that 'everything' has been put under him [Christ], it is clear that this does not include God himself, who put everything under Christ. When he [Christ] has done this, then the Son himself will be made subject to him [the Father] who put everything under him, so that God [the Father] may be all in all. (Brackets added.)

The end to which Paul refers in 1 Corinthians 15:24 is the transition point between the Millennium and the eternal state, at which time Jesus will return headship over all creation to the Father, and forever thereafter the Father will reign supreme, with Christ seated at His right hand.

Resistance Is Futile

Surprisingly, during the Millennium, the world's spiritual climate—excluding in Israel—will gradually decline rather than become stronger. This will occur as a steady number of children who are born during the Millennium do not turn to Christ in saving faith. As the centuries pass, the number of unsaved individuals living in the world will very likely burgeon into millions of unredeemed men and women. Although Satan will not be present to incite outright rebellion against Christ until near the end of Millennium, these unbelievers will likely begin to resent Christ's strict rule over them long before Satan is released from the Abyss, and they will crave to be set free from it. If this development seems inconceivable to you, remember that Adam and Eve disobeyed God despite their having an intimate relationship with Him in the Garden of Eden. Because of their disobedience, all humans now possess a sin nature, and none of us needs provocation by Satan in order to do evil. This reality will be demonstrated in unbelievers throughout the world in the Millennium.

In Psalm 2, King David describes the contempt for the king of Israel held by the nations that once surrounded God's people. Because Psalm 2 is a millennial psalm, David's words carry a double meaning and convey a thinly veiled allusion to future unbelievers' antipathy toward Christ's governance in the Millennium.

> Why do the nations conspire and the peoples plot in vain? The kings of the earth take their stand and the rulers gather together against the LORD and against his Anointed One. "Let us break their chains," they say, "and throw off their fetters." (vv. 1–3)

God will respond to sedition on the part of the nations with both amusement and derision.

> The One enthroned in heaven laughs; the Lord scoffs at them. Then he rebukes them in his anger and terrifies them in his wrath, saying, "I have installed my King on Zion, my holy hill." (vv. 4–6)

Christ will meet all rebellion against Him in the Millennium with shock and awe, and every crime and infraction of His laws will be summarily punished. In Isaiah 66:24, God says worshippers from around the world "'will go out and look upon the dead bodies of those who rebelled against me; their worm will not die, nor will their fire be quenched, and they will be loathsome to all mankind.'" Unlike today, when rogue nations often evade justice and continue to commit atrocities with impunity, in that day, all defiance of Christ's authority on the part of nations will be met with swift and severe retribution. With crushing force, He will visit justice upon all who violate His commands or challenge His authority.

Psalm 2 concludes with a warning to all who resist Christ's rule during the Millennium:

> Therefore, you kings, be wise; be warned, you rulers of the earth. Serve the LORD with fear and rejoice with trembling. Kiss the Son, lest he be angry and you be destroyed in your way, for his wrath can flare up in a moment. Blessed are all who take refuge in him. (vv. 10–12)

Significantly, in no place does Scripture indicate that Christ will conscript or otherwise maintain armed forces during the Millennium or that He will impose His authority by means of military might. Instead, Isaiah 2:4 and Micah 4:3 indicate the very opposite, saying all weapons of warfare on earth will be destroyed at the outset of the Millennium. So how will Christ preserve order and deal with nations that resist Him? He will do so directly and with His own divine power, including by bringing devastating droughts and plagues upon nations that do not comply with His commands (Zechariah 14:17–18).

In promising ancient Israel safety from its enemies, God declares, "'The LORD will grant that the enemies who rise up against you will be defeated before you. They will come at you from one direction but flee from you in seven'" (Deuteronomy 28:7). Notice God does not say Israel's enemies would be defeated *by* Israel but rather *before* Israel. It seems reasonable to assume that God will keep this promise to Israel in the Millennium by unilaterally defeating their enemies as they stand by and watch.

Therefore, as we think of Christ's millennial government, we should not envision a military regime that dispatches armed forces to keep order in conquered lands. Instead, we should anticipate that Christ Himself, or the Father on Christ's behalf, will need only to speak in order to uphold justice and subdue His enemies. All of this will come about as a result of the Father's own sovereign pledge to make Christ's enemies His "footstool" (Psalm 110:1) and to make Christ the supreme Majesty of all the earth.

Saints of State

Christ's government will be administrated largely or entirely by resurrected saints who reign under Him. Scripture indicates that if you are a born-again believer when you exit this life, you will participate in some capacity in the millennial government. In Revelation 20:4, the apostle John says,

> I saw thrones on which were seated those who had been given authority to judge. And I saw the souls of those who had been beheaded because of their testimony for Jesus and because of the word of God. They had not worshiped the beast or his image and had not received his mark on their foreheads or their hands. They came to life and reigned with Christ a thousand years.

John is describing believers who will have been converted to Christ during the Tribulation and also died during it, and who are then raised to life at the Second Coming and given positions of authority in Christ's global government. These glorified believers will exercise their rule under allegiance to Christ, so some interpreters have described their roles as "vassal kingships,"[51] subordinate to Christ who is "King of Kings and Lord of Lords" (1 Timothy 6:15).

Other Scriptures indicate that Christ will grant measures of authority to all resurrected believers, rather than only to those who will have died during the Tribulation. In Daniel 7:27, Daniel's angelic interpreter foretells a future time when "the sovereignty, power and greatness of the kingdoms under the whole heaven will be handed over to the saints, the people of the Most High." In the New

Testament, Paul says to the believers at Corinth, "Do you not know that the saints will judge the world?" (1 Corinthians 6:2). Since all persons who put true saving faith in God are saints, including Old and New Testament believers, this suggests that every child of God who will have ever lived will participate to some degree in the governance of Christ's millennial kingdom! This truth is also either stated explicitly or alluded to in Revelation 3:21, 5:10, 20:4, 6, and 22:5.

What work will Christ assign to us when we reign with Him in His earthly kingdom? Scripture answers some but not all of our questions, and we must tread cautiously in filling in the gaps with our own speculations. In Jesus's Parable of the Ten Minas in Luke 19:11–27, the master grants to his servants authority over various numbers of cities in proportion to how profitably each of them invested his money. One purpose of that parable is to encourage believers to live faithfully to Christ in this life by assuring us He will reward us with roles of authority in His kingdom.

Depending upon how literally one interprets the details of Christ's Parable of the Ten Minas, it seems clear that our present faithfulness will be the determining factor as to the extent of authority we are given, since some servants in the parable are set in charge of more cities than others. As to our specific duties, Scripture contains little information. In 1 Corinthians 6:2–3, the apostle Paul reminds the believers at Corinth that "the saints will judge the world" and that "we will judge angels." The word Paul uses in these verses translated "judge" in some English versions can mean judging in a judicial sense by adjudicating cases as in a court of law, and it can also mean "to administer affairs, to govern." Most likely, we will be engaged in some combination of both. As for believers who do little for Christ in this present life and enter eternity "as one escaping through the flames" (1 Corinthians 3:15)—*by the skin of their teeth* as it has otherwise been phrased—we can trust that God will wisely place them in roles corresponding to the extent of their present faithfulness. Of course, we should keep in mind that all positions of authority and service in the millennial kingdom will be undeserved by those to whom they are graciously granted.

Gentile believers will govern Gentile nations and perhaps will participate in ensuring that justice is served when nations under their jurisdiction resist His authority. Because Christ's government will extend globally, it will provide ample room for all of God's resurrected people who will have ever lived to rule over their assigned territories. Perhaps we will be allocated authority over areas of greater or lesser size and distinction based upon the quality of our present service and the degree to which we now sacrifice and suffer for Christ.

What Paul meant when he said believers will judge angels is a bit mysterious because Paul does not elaborate on it, and it is not mentioned any place else in Scripture. Some interpreters take Paul to mean God will authorize believers to pass sentence upon fallen angels. If this is the case, it will happen only once at the end of the Millennium when Satan is cast into the lake of fire (Revelation 20:7–10). I find it more conceivable that God will confer authority upon believers to oversee the holy angels during the Millennium and throughout eternity.

Preachers and Bible teachers sometimes remark that believers now on earth are "training for reigning" as we serve Christ and obey His commands. While we may find such a thought inspirational, the fact is whatever skills and expertise we may possess in this life will not prepare us for the enormous responsibilities we will shoulder in the Millennium. God will impart upon us supernatural competencies to reign in glorious seats of honor in our Lord's kingdom when we are transformed into the likeness of Christ (1 John 3:2). Therefore, if you are like me and at times have difficulty balancing your checkbook, do not fret over the prospect of being responsible for leading an entire city or region. Christ will equip you for whatever tasks He assigns to you!

Some believers' giftedness, education, and experience would seem to make them well suited for high positions of leadership in the

Millennium, but these are the exception. Most believers throughout history have come from humble backgrounds and were not standouts in terms of their abilities or achievements. In 1 Corinthians 1:26, Paul noted that most members of the church at Corinth did not come from the upper classes of society: "Not many of you were wise by human standards; not many were influential; not many were of noble birth." And yet Paul affirmed that these same believers will one day be given exalted positions of leadership in Christ's kingdom (1 Corinthians 6:2–3).

In the Millennium and in the eternal state that comes after it, believers will be granted authority to rule that is commensurate with their faithfulness and willingness to suffer for Christ in this life. Our rank in Christ's government will in no way be determined by our present intelligence, giftedness, or experience. Paul declares in 1 Corinthians 1:27, "God chose the foolish things of the world to shame the wise; [and] God chose the weak things of the world to shame the strong."

I believe many of the highest offices in Christ's future government will go to believers whom the world will never have heard of but who will have remained loyal to Christ despite having endured hostility, deprivation, imprisonment, and even martyrdom. Some positions will be awarded to missionaries who shared the Gospel under grueling conditions on lonely, distant fields, and to pastors who put in long hours of ministry, faithfully proclaiming God's Word to small congregations with little recompense or acknowledgment. Many ranks of leadership will be filled by Christian housewives and schoolteachers and office clerks and salespersons who "bloomed where they were planted," made sacrifices, and walked by faith. At His Second Coming, Christ will call such saints to the head of the line and award them abundantly for their faithfulness. "See, the Sovereign LORD comes with power, and his arm rules for him. See, his reward is with him, and his recompense accompanies him" (Isaiah 40:10).

Believers who will have followed Christ with unflagging

faithfulness "will be called great in the kingdom of heaven" (Matthew 5:19), while others will be called least. Believers who will have lived less faithfully and suffered for Christ less severely will be awarded for whatever merits they earned, but they will receive less distinguished roles in Christ's kingdom.

Regardless of our station in this life or what we will have done for Christ, our glorification in the Millennium will come as an unmerited gift graciously bestowed upon us by God, "in order that in the coming ages he might show the incomparable riches of his grace, expressed in his kindness to us in Christ Jesus" (Ephesians 2:7). As someone has wisely observed, "It is not great men who change the world, but weak men in the hands of a great God."[52]

Israel's Role in Christ's Millennial Government

Nineteenth-century Scottish minister and hymn writer Horatius Bonar called Israel "the great nation of the future." In the Millennium, God will keep His promise to make Israel preeminent over all nations of the earth and the sole spiritual, political, and economic superpower of the international community, with Jerusalem established as the world's capital (Jeremiah 3:17; Micah 4:2). Even in our own day, Israel continually dominates the world's attention. George Gilder has strikingly observed, "The central issue in international politics, dividing the world into two fractious armies, is the tiny state of Israel."[53] In the Millennium, God's exaltation of the Israelis will cause "All who see them [to] acknowledge that they are a people the LORD has blessed" (Isaiah 61:9).

Because of Israel's prominence in the Millennium, the highest political offices in Christ's kingdom will exist in the Israeli government. Long ago, Jesus promised these premier positions to His disciples who followed Him during His earthly ministry—save for Judas, whose place will presumably be filled by Matthias, the disciple chosen to replace Judas after he betrayed Christ and committed suicide (Acts 1:15–26). Jesus said to His disciples in Matthew 19:28, "'I tell you the truth, at the renewal of all things, when the Son of Man sits on his glorious throne, you who have followed me will also sit on twelve thrones, judging the twelve tribes of Israel.'" Evidently there is no greater reward God can grant to Christ's first disciples than headship over their own beloved nation in Christ's eternal kingdom!

When this promise is brought to fruition in the Millennium, it will simultaneously fulfill an earlier promise made by God to the nation of Israel through the prophet Isaiah: "'I will restore your judges as in days of old, your counselors as at the beginning'" (Isaiah 1:26). Israel's judges were those who ruled the nation prior to the institution of Israel's monarchy, and Jesus's twelve disciples will perhaps inherit those roles in the Millennium.

In Daniel 7:27, an angel explained to Daniel that in the future, "'the sovereignty, power and greatness of the kingdoms under the whole heaven will be handed over to the saints, the people of the Most High. His kingdom will be an everlasting kingdom, and all rulers will worship and obey him.'"

When we try to imagine geopolitics in the Millennium, we may wonder whether nations that will have existed in history will also exist in the Millennium. Will there be a United States of America then? Will there be a Brazil, England, or Japan? When Christ returns in the Second Coming, most of the earth will have been laid waste during the Great Tribulation, and mortal believers who enter the kingdom will be like Noah and his family members disembarking from the ark into the desolated postflood world in which nothing is the same as it was. Many of the early years of the Millennium will probably be taken up by a vast redevelopment of civilization. Whether all of the nations that will have existed prior to the apocalypse will continue in the Millennium is an open question. Some, including Egypt, Assyria, Philistia, Ethiopia, and Edom, apparently will because they are mentioned by name in millennial prophecies.

Most of the world's ethnicities will probably carry on into the Millennium, and members of various nationalities will likely regroup and reestablish vestiges of their societies. According to John Walvoord,

> It is an error, however, to assume that national identity will be lost in eternity. Just as there will be individual identity, so also there will be racial identity, and individuals will inevitably carry throughout eternity an identification related to some extent to their place in the history of the world. Hence, Israelites will be Israelites throughout eternity and Gentiles will be Gentiles was well.[54]

Many glimpses of life in Christ's millennial kingdom given in the Bible probably pertain exclusively to Israel. One example, found in Isaiah 32:1–8, describes the righteousness and integrity that will distinguish the people of Israel during the Millennium. "See, a king will reign in righteousness and rulers will rule with justice" (32:1). The noble and upright character of Israel's leaders will pervade Israel's entire society, and "Each man will be like a shelter from the wind and a refuge from the storm, like streams of water in the desert and the shadow of a great rock in a thirsty land" (32:2). Israel's righteousness and integrity will serve a model for societies and cultures the world over. Nineteenth-century author Henry David Thoreau wrote, "I please myself with imagining a State at least which can afford to be just to all men." Millennial Israel will embody that ideal.

As the world's seat of government, Israel will likely dictate global affairs and monitor national undertakings and relationships. Resistance to Israel's hegemony and even the slightest hint of aggression toward it will bring harsh reprisal from the Messiah. In Isaiah 49:23, the Lord declares to Israel that kings and queens "'will bow down before you with their faces to the ground; they will lick the dust at your feet. Then you will know that I am the LORD; those who hope in me will not be disappointed.'" Israel's borders will at last enfold all of the land God promised to Abraham and his descendants, and everlasting peace, prosperity, and global supremacy will bless the nation. All of these blessings will come from Israel's glorious Messiah-King:

> Of the increase of his government and peace there will be no end. He will reign on David's throne and over his kingdom, establishing and upholding it with justice and righteousness from that time on and forever. The zeal of the LORD Almighty will accomplish this. (Isaiah 9:7)

Looking for That Blessed Hope

Some of us are old enough to remember Andy Williams, the silken-voiced tenor who was widely known for his Christmas specials on television in the sixties through the eighties. Williams sang the title song for the 1968 movie *Romeo and Juliet* called "A Time for Us," a line of which goes like this:

> A time for us someday there'll be
> A new world, a world of shining hope for you and me.[55]

Andy Williams was not singing about the millennial reign of Christ, but those lyrics do describe the bright and certain future of every believer. In this chapter, we have seen that Christ's future kingdom will indeed usher in a world of shining hope that His people will enjoy with Him forever. Satan's rule on earth will end, and Jesus will reign with absolute authority and perfect righteousness in a global government that is free of corruption and that provides peace, justice, and prosperity to its citizens.

How should we respond to this awesome revelation of what awaits us? Wisdom dictates that we obey Paul's instructions in Titus 2:12–13 "to say 'No' to ungodliness and worldly passions, and to live self-controlled, upright and godly lives in this present age, while we wait for the blessed hope—the glorious appearing of our great God and Savior, Jesus Christ." Since our eternal future will be shaped by how well or poorly we obey that command, nothing we do in this life could be more worthwhile.

5

You in the Millennium

> But we know that when he appears, we shall be like him, for we shall see him as he is.
>
> —1 John 3:2

In September 1971, John Lennon's wildly popular song "Imagine"[56] was released and quickly skyrocketed to global acclaim. It went on to became one of the best-selling singles in history. In 2004, *Rolling Stone* magazine placed it third in the magazine's "500 Greatest Songs of All Time." In the song, Lennon envisions an idyllic world undivided by political boundaries and free of hunger, violence, social strife, and religion, where the peoples of earth are enabled to live in peace and harmony. Lennon's song has since become the international mantra for social liberalism and existentialist ideology. New Year's Eve event organizers have played it to the sway of misty-eyed listeners just before the Times Square ball drops in New York City.

The world of the Millennium will bear some resemblances to the one Lennon visualized—excluding of course the absence of religion. Christ's global kingdom will unite all nations on earth under one benevolent Head, and social evils that have vexed humankind throughout history will be eradicated. With the exception of instances in which Christ disciplines wayward nations, wars, plagues, starvation, natural disasters, and their like will exist only in history books—if even there! Humanity itself will experience dramatic changes for the better. In this chapter, we will explore what Scripture reveals about those changes and their impact upon humankind when Christ rules the earth.

A Perfect You

From Adam and Eve to the present, millions of human beings have exercised faith to become children of God, and every one of those believers will return and live on earth during the Millennium, including you. Whether you leave this world by way of your death or are caught up to heaven at the Rapture, you will return to earth with them, and with Christ, at the Second Coming. Resurrected and raptured believers will have lived in heaven for periods of time when Christ returns, and all will possess immortal bodies.

What will your immortal body be like? Another way to put the question is, what will *you* be like during the Millennium? You will possess a physical body, an intellect, and a will—all the aspects of personhood and individuality that distinguish you as an individual now—but everything about you will have been made perfect. Let's take a deeper look at what Scripture says about your resurrected body.

To be sure, your body will be your own body—the one you possess right now. The fact that your body will have been resurrected as opposed to replaced makes this certain. Paul says, "He who raised Christ from the dead will also give life to *your mortal bodies*" (Romans 8:11). Commenting upon 1 Corinthians 15:38, John MacArthur explains,

> Our resurrected bodies as believers will have a continuity with the bodies we have now. Our bodies

> will die and they will change form, but they will still be *our* bodies.[57]

Although your body will be the same one that you indwell in this life, God will bestow upon it some remarkable upgrades to make it suitable not only for the Millennium but also for eternity thereafter. In 1 Corinthians 15:51–52, the apostle Paul says, "Listen, I tell you a mystery: We will not all sleep,"—meaning will not all experience physical death—"but we will all be changed"—a reference to the supernatural transformation of our physical bodies—"in a flash, in the twinkling of an eye, at the last trumpet. For the trumpet will sound, the dead will be raised imperishable, and we will be changed. For the perishable must clothe itself with the imperishable, and the mortal with immortality." Paul is telling us that the resurrection of believers will happen simultaneously with the Rapture, and whether you die or are taken to heaven in the Rapture, your body will undergo the same supernatural transformation.

In 1 Corinthians 15:35–58, Paul describes the believer's resurrected body with emphasis upon how it differs from our current mortal bodies. He says the believer's resurrected body is "imperishable," meaning it will be unsusceptible to disease, the ravages of age, or death. Your body will be made physically immortal and set free from its sin nature, just as your soul is now spiritually immortal and set free from bondage to sin.[58] In Romans 8:23, Paul calls this transformation "the redemption of our bodies." In your immortal body, you will never experience physical suffering, sickness, or infirmity but will enjoy perfect health and vitality forever.

In 1 Corinthians 15, Paul continues His description of the majesty and splendor of our resurrected body even further by centering upon two concepts that will apply to them—glory and power. "Glory" carries the idea of holy splendor and magnificence, and perhaps also a visible radiance similar to what Christ's body displayed at the Transfiguration (Matthew 17:1–2). "Power" speaks of the invincibility, resilience, and spiritual fortitude our bodies will possess.

As if all of these amazing blessings were not enough to convince us of the grandeur of our resurrected bodies, Paul goes on to say they will bear similarities to Jesus's own resurrected body (1 Corinthians 15:49)! In Philippians 3:21, Paul says Christ "will transform our lowly bodies so that they will be like His glorious body." What an astounding fact this is! The apostle John repeats this same truth in 1 John 3:2, "Dear friends, now we are children of God, and what we will be has not yet been made known. But we know that when he appears, we shall be like him, for we shall see him as he is."

Theologian J. I. Packer explains it this way:

> Jesus was the first to rise from the dead, and when he returns to this world he will raise his servants to a resurrection life like his own. Christians alive at his coming will undergo a marvelous transformation, while Christians who had died will experience a glorious re-embodiment. The bodies Christians possess now are at best poor tools for expressing the desires and purposes of regenerate hearts, and many of the weaknesses with which the saints struggle—shyness, shortness of temper, lust, depression, coolness in relationships, and so on—are closely linked with our physical constitution and its patterning in our behavior. The bodies that become ours in the general resurrection will be bodies that perfectly match our regenerate characters and will prove perfect instruments for our holy self-expression throughout eternity.[59]

It will help in understanding the nature of your glorified body in the Millennium to study physical descriptions of Jesus in the New Testament as He appeared while He remained on earth during the forty days between His resurrection and His ascension, and also descriptions of His appearance in heaven.

The Gospels indicate that some aspects of Jesus's resurrected body were similar to any normal human body, while others were very different. After Jesus's resurrection, His body was still composed of "flesh and bones" (Luke 24:39) and was recognizable by those who knew Him (John 20:16). He could consume food (Luke 24:42–43), and His body retained the scars of His crucifixion (Luke 24:39; John 20:27). However, He could now pass through solid walls and move from place to place instantaneously (Luke 24:31; John 20:19).

Although Christ was raised from the grave with an immortal body, while He remained on earth prior to His ascension to heaven, it did not possess—or did not appear to possess—some of the supernatural qualities described in visions of Him in His heavenly glory. However, His body apparently underwent even further transformations when He ascended back to heaven.

At Jesus's Transfiguration, Peter, James, and John beheld His form in which He had existed from eternity past, and which He resumed after returning to heaven. Matthew 17:2 records that, when Christ was transfigured, "His face shone like the sun, and his clothes became as white as the light." This description bears striking similarities to visions of the preincarnate Christ given to Ezekiel (Ezekiel 1:27–28), to Daniel (Daniel 7:9), and to the apostle John (Revelation 4:3). Astonishingly, Scripture declares that your body will possess these very same characteristics!

During the Millennium, you and other resurrected believers will live on earth among mortal human beings as glorified children of God. Your appearance will, no doubt, astound flesh-and-blood human beings who encounter you, and it will visibly confirm of the reality of resurrection and the value of faith in Christ. Speaking of resurrected believers' glorified bodies, C. S. Lewis wrote, "the dullest and most uninteresting person you can talk to may one day be a creature which, if you saw it now, you would be strongly tempted to worship."[60]

Despite all these incredible enhancements, you will still be you, and passages in both the Old and New Testament indicate resurrected believers will a be able to recognize one other. Samuel the prophet retained his earthly appearance after his death (1 Samuel 28:13–14). Moses and Elijah apparently bore a semblance of their mortal appearances when they appeared at Christ's Transfiguration (Matthew 17:3). Abraham and Lazarus were recognizable to the rich man in Christ's story of the rich man and Lazarus (Luke 16:23–24), and as mentioned already, Jesus was recognizable to those who saw him after His resurrection (Matthew 28:16–20; Mark 16:12–13; John 20:24–28).

This strongly suggests that you will retain at least some aspects of your present physical appearance, minus any defects or disabilities that will be erased forever. Do you now have to wear corrective lenses in order to read this book, as I do? One day you will enjoy perfect eyesight. Do you strain now to discern sounds and voices around you, as I do? Prepare to enjoy excellent hearing. Do you suffer from constant pain or suffer physical limitations that bar you from activities you enjoy? Prepare to say goodbye to all of those infirmities one day. You are scheduled for a total makeover!

In an oracle on the Millennium, the prophet Isaiah states, "Then will the eyes of the blind be opened and the ears of the deaf unstopped. Then will the lame leap like a deer, and the mute tongue shout for joy" (Isaiah 35:5–6).

Certainly there is much we cannot know now about the exact nature of our future glorified bodies, but Scripture reveals enough details to spark great hope and anticipation in our hearts over what God has in store for us. Whatever physical, mental, and spiritual blessings await you in the Millennium, you may be sure they will far exceed what you can imagine now. You will discover that those grandeurs will make whatever sufferings your allegiance to Christ may cost you in this life exceedingly worthwhile. Paul said he considered "that our present sufferings are not worth comparing with the glory that will be revealed in us" (Romans 8:18). The apostle John states simply, "what we will be has not yet been made known" (1 John 3:2). In the meantime, it is enough for us to know and cherish what God's Word does reveal to us about our future state. One day, you will be like Christ! No brighter future could be possible!

Your New Nature

Beyond enhancing your physical appearance, abilities, and mental capacity, becoming like Christ will also include a transformation of your character. God will make you like Jesus down to the very core of your being. Yet, in this life, even the most spiritually mature believers fall far short of that ideal. Every one of us who belong to Jesus must admit, in the words of the hymn writer, "Prone to wander, Lord I feel it, Prone to leave the God I love."[61] We are redeemed, but in our flesh, we are still woefully imperfect.

Perhaps you have read Romans 7 and related personally to Paul's frustration over his inability to live in conformity to God's commands. Like Paul, you want to please God in every way, but none of us can do that perfectly. We can go for only so long before we slip into sin and find ourselves needing to ask God's forgiveness. In exasperation, Paul says, "What a wretched man I am! Who will rescue me from this body of death?" (Romans 7:24). He was referring to his present physical body that is unredeemed, prone to sin, and incapable of moral or spiritual perfection. Then, in answer to his own question, he adds, "Thanks be to God—through Jesus Christ our Lord! So then, I myself in my mind am a slave to God's law, but in the sinful nature a slave to the law of sin." Paul knew that only Jesus could make him like Jesus!

Paul also knew that one day he would receive a resurrected body that possesses no sin nature, and the same will happen for you. You will be made sinless the moment you die, or are raptured, and enter heaven, and your ability to live in absolute righteousness will continue when you return to live on earth forever in your glorified body.

Try to envision never experiencing the daily battle with temptation that relentlessly occupies your waking hours today. You will never fail to please God in any way, because the very idea of disobedience to His commands will not occur to you. Besetting sins that you wrestle with now will not attract you at all then. Imagine what a delightful and refreshing feeling of total liberation that will bring! Although in your present state, as a regenerate believer in Christ, you possess the mind of Christ (1 Corinthians 2:16), and the Holy Spirit lives within you, you still retain your fleshly, sinful nature, and the Spirit and the flesh are at war with each other within you (Galatians 5:17). In eternity, you will shed your sin nature, and you will no longer struggle with a body and a nature that are prone to disobedience. Although you will share the very glory of Christ, you will never know pride or feel inclined to gloat over your abilities or accomplishments. It is then that you will finally know "the glorious freedom of the children of God" (Romans 8:21). As I once heard Billy Graham say in a crusade sermon, "I look forward to that day, because I sin every day."

Your Abilities

Your glorified body will be equipped with incredible abilities that we cannot even imagine now, and you will need such abilities in order to function in the roles assigned to you by Christ. One of the many blessings enjoyed by resurrected believers in the Millennium will be the gift of leadership, for as we have already seen, believers in their glorified bodies will be entrusted with high positions of authority over cities and territories as rewards for their faithfulness to Christ in this life.[62] Supernatural aptitudes will be required in order for glorified believers to oversee commerce, manage governmental affairs, and carry out other duties under the headship of Christ. Your intellect will likely be greatly increased, and you will be blessed with supernatural wisdom that equips you to discharge your responsibilities.

Your Relationships

All three synoptic Gospels (Matthew, Mark, and Luke) tell the story of a group of Sadducees who came to Jesus, intending to trap Him with a trick question. Unlike the ultraconservative Pharisees, Sadducees were theological liberals who denied the reality of the afterlife. They presented their question to Jesus in a silly story of a woman who married seven brothers, one after another, and all the brothers died. The group asked Jesus, "'Now then, at the resurrection whose wife will she be, since the seven brothers were married to her?'" (Luke 20:33). Jesus's response not only shut down the Sadducees' scheme, but it also answered a question asked by many believers today: will there be marriage in heaven?

> [He] replied, "The people of this age marry and are given in marriage. But those who are considered worthy of taking part in that age and in the resurrection from the dead will neither marry nor be given in marriage, and they can no longer die; for they are like the angels. They are God's children, since they are children of the resurrection." (Luke 20:34–36)

By "that age," Jesus was referring to the Millennium and eternity after it, and He said resurrected believers in it will not marry, nor will their earthly marriages continue beyond this life. This is because procreation will be unnecessary and because we will not need the gratification and companionship we now seek through marital relationships.

If you are a happily married Christian, you probably find this news disappointing. You may not believe heaven, or life on earth in eternity, can be joyful for you without your husband or wife. God understands such feelings, as do all of us who are blessed with good marriages. But you need not be saddened or have your expectations of heaven dashed by this truth. In eternity, you will not need marriage to dispel loneliness or to give your life meaning. In eternity, you will feel utterly complete in Christ in ways you cannot imagine now. You will no longer be subject to loneliness or isolation, but you will instead live in absolute joy, peace, and contentment throughout eternity because of your oneness with Christ. Randy Alcorn explains this truth well:

> The one-flesh marital union we know on Earth is a signpost pointing to our relationship with Christ as our bridegroom. Once we reach the destination, the signpost becomes unnecessary. That one marriage—our marriage to Christ—will be so completely satisfying that even the most wonderful earthly marriage couldn't be as fulfilling.[63]

On such matters, we must simply trust God to keep His word and make eternity the experience of total fulfillment, joy, and peace God's Word assures us it will be for every believer. Whatever the afterlife holds for you and all of God's children, not a single part of it will disappoint you. Every aspect of it will exceed your wildest expectations, and you will never long to return to life as it was for you on earth.

Little is said in Scripture about human relationships other than marriage, but the details given about marriage provide at least a baseline for speculating about how we will relate to other relatives, friends, and acquaintances in heaven and in the Millennium. As with our spouses, we will likely recognize others we have known on earth but will not have the same relationships with them we experienced in our mortal existence. In eternity, every glorified believer will enjoy a depth of companionship with every other glorified believer that exceeds the happiest marriages in this life. John MacArthur says, "If having such a deep relationship with your spouse here is too wonderful, imagine how glorious it will be to enjoy a perfect relationship with every human in the whole expanse of heaven—forever!"[64]

The apostle Paul sums up our entire experience of eternity by saying, "and so shall we ever be with the Lord" (1 Thessalonians 4:17). More than anything else, heaven, the Millennium, and eternity beyond it will center upon our presence with Jesus. All the earthly relationships we leave behind will pale in comparison with the incomparable joy of spending eternity in the presence of Christ. No other relationship on heaven or on earth could come close to matching our blessed union with our Lord Jesus.

When our boys were youngsters, Lee Ann and I took them on their first visit to Disney World in Orlando, Florida. They had never experienced anything bigger than the county fair and could not possibly imagine the Magic Kingdom, no matter how vividly we described it. We drove down and rented a hotel room, then got up the next morning and piled into the car for our big day at the famous resort. On our way, we drove past a McDonalds that sported a huge indoor play area that could be seen clearly from the road. When our boys caught sight of it, they begged frantically for us to stop so they could play in it. We tried to tell them that something much better was coming, but they cried alligator tears when we kept driving, because they had played in many McDonalds but had never experienced Disney World.

When it comes to choosing between life on earth and life in eternity, I suspect many believers prefer McDonalds over Disney World. This life is familiar to them, but the next life is mysterious and maybe even a little frightening. We may wish eternity would allow us to carry on our lives here, with our present surroundings, relationships, and activities remaining unchanged forever. Will we like heaven? Will we live in eternal loneliness if our connections with family and friends differ there? The answer is a resounding no! If only we knew what God has in store!

After one hour in Disney World, our sons forgot all about McDonalds, and I don't think that the golden arches ever had the same appeal for them again. A similar change of heart will happen in you when you step into eternity. You will not yearn for your previous life on earth and pine away for what you left behind. We are told we have to give up in order to go up, but once you arrive on the other side, you will realize that you have given up nothing at all. C. S. Lewis forcefully observed our inclination to settle for less than God's best: "We are half-hearted creatures, fooling about with drink and sex and ambition when infinite joy is offered us, like an ignorant child who wants to go on making mud pies in a slum because he cannot imagine what is meant by the offer of a holiday at the sea. We are far too easily pleased."[65]

6

Worship in the Millennium

> [Jesus will come] to be glorified in his holy people and to be marveled at among all those who have believed. This includes you, because you believed our testimony to you.
>
> —2 Thessalonians 1:10

The apostle Paul had the Millennium in mind when he wrote to the Philippian church and told them that one day, "at the name of Jesus every knee [will] bow, in heaven and on earth and under the earth, and every tongue confess that Jesus Christ is Lord, to the glory of God the Father" (Philippians 2:10–11). In the Millennium, worshipping Jesus will dominate life on earth and will become the apex activity of every tribe and tongue as all human beings, mortal and immortal, give praise to Christ wholeheartedly and without ceasing. At that time, idolatry and false worship will not be tolerated (Zechariah 13:1–6). Christianity will not be one of many world religions but the only religion, and "the earth will be filled with the knowledge of the glory of the LORD, as the waters cover the sea" (Habakkuk 2:14).

Today, only 35 percent of the world's population claims to be Christian,[66] and even that number is probably greatly inflated by the overly broad definition of "Christian" used by most pollsters. This means at least six out of ten people on earth don't even profess to be Christians. In contrast, at the start of the Millennium, 100 percent of people on earth will be genuine believers in Christ, and although unbelievers will gradually multiply, the number of atheists will remain zero!

How will worship in the Millennium differ from ways in which true believers worship today? Will houses of worship exist where congregations gather to sing to God, hear choirs perform, and listen to pastors preach? Will believers attend Bible studies? Will any of the worship songs believers cherish today be sung then? Some forms of present-day Christian worship will probably continue into eternity, but Scripture signals that the Millennium will bring major changes in how God's people exalt Him. Most significantly, all worship will be authentic and heartfelt, energized by Christ's physical presence on earth.

Full Disclosure

Try to imagine the awe and wonder that will burst from within you over the sight of Jesus seated on His throne in Jerusalem! Scripture clearly implies Christ will possess a literal—albeit glorified—body that can be seen and touched, and He evidently will radiate with brilliant light. When Jesus gave Peter, James, and John a glimpse of His true appearance at His Transfiguration, John testifies that "His face shone like the sun, and his clothes became as white as the light" (Matthew 17:2). This account bears similarity to Ezekiel's vision of the preincarnate Christ, in which the prophet sees a manlike figure and says, "I saw that from what appeared to be his waist up he looked like glowing metal, as if full of fire, and that from there down he looked like fire; and brilliant light surrounded him" (Ezekiel 1:27). Similarly, in a vision of Christ in heaven given to the apostle John on the Island of Patmos, John says, "his eyes were like blazing fire.

His feet were like bronze glowing in a furnace" (Revelation 1:14–15). Both of these men beheld the unveiled Christ of eternity, the very One whom we will worship throughout the Millennium and forever after it!

Believers who die are blessed to look upon Jesus continually in heaven, but they may find it even more satisfying to finally see Christ enthroned in His millennial temple, in fulfillment of all Old and New Testament promises of an earthly kingdom reigned over by the Messiah. In the words of an old gospel song, "What a day, glorious day, that will be"!

Our worship of Christ during the Millennium will become far deeper and more exhilarating when God vastly enlarges our capacity to understand Him and His ways. In Isaiah 55:9, God says to all humankind, "As the heavens are higher than the earth, so are my ways higher than your ways and my thoughts than your thoughts." Our present mortal minds cannot process God's infinitely superior thoughts any more than a grasshopper can grasp Einstein's theory of relativity, but in eternity, we will be enabled to.

In 1 Corinthians 13:12, Paul contrasts our present knowledge of eternal realities with the expanded awareness we will possess in eternity: "Now we see but a poor reflection as in a mirror; then we shall see face to face. Now I know in part; then I shall know fully, even as I am fully known." When we receive our resurrected bodies, our spiritual IQ will shoot through the roof, and every aspect of God's divine nature, His purposes, and His ways will suddenly become crystal clear to us!

Our dramatically heightened grasp of the mysteries of God will enrich our worship in ways we cannot anticipate or even conceive now. Just as a toddler who is taken by his parents to visit the Lincoln Memorial in Washington, DC, cannot possibly perceive or appreciate the historical significance of the man whose presidency is memorialized there, we as mortal believers now worship an infinitely majestic God with a woefully limited perception of His divine nature and power. Not so for resurrected believers in the Millennium! We will praise our Lord with full awareness of who He is, and our worship will take on dimensions of grandeur that leave us awestruck and hungry for more.

Worship of God will also become more profound for believers who are still in their mortal bodies during the Millennium. Every mortal on earth will see Christ with their own eyes and will be taught by Him (Isaiah 2:3; 54:13). These experiences will produce a depth of insight and spiritual understanding unlike anything the world has ever known. John Walvoord says,

> Christ as the world ruler of the millennial kingdom will be the object of worship, and the universal instruction in Biblical truth, as well as the many demonstrations of divine power and the abundant ministry of the Holy Spirit, will foster a spiritual life on a world-wide scale unprecedented in the history of the world.[67]

Zephaniah 2:11 says, "The nations on every shore will worship him, every one in its own land." People from every corner of the world will also travel to Jerusalem to see Jesus and sit under His tutelage. Isaiah 66:23 reveals that "'From one New Moon to another and from one Sabbath to another, all mankind will come and bow down before me' says the LORD." The prophet Micah also foretells these international pilgrimages:

> Many nations will come and say, "Come, let us go up to the mountain of the LORD, to the house of the God of Jacob. He will teach us his ways, so that we may walk in his paths." The law will go out from Zion, the word of the LORD from Jerusalem. (Micah 4:2)

Israel's airports and seaports will become the world's busiest travel centers, and because of Christ's physical presence in Jerusalem, the city will bear a new name: "The Lord is There" (Ezekiel 48:35).

Undistracted Worship

With Satan out of the way during the Millennium, worship on earth will become like worship in heaven—entirely pure and free of Satan's meddling. It has been said truthfully that Satan never misses a church service. He shows up wherever Christ is worshipped, seeking to sow seeds of doubt, confusion, and division. Satan also continually attempts to sabotage human efforts to share the Gospel with unbelievers. Jesus said in His Parable of the Soils that, in the present age, "When anyone hears the message about the kingdom and does not understand it, the evil one comes and snatches away what was sown in his heart" (Matthew 13:19). Paul says Satan blinds the minds of unbelievers (2 Corinthians 4:4). All such interference by Satan and his demons will disappear in Christ's earthly kingdom.

Illumination by the Holy Spirit

Several passages in the Old Testament foretell a special outpouring of the Holy Spirit during the Millennium (Isaiah 32:15; 44:3; Ezekiel 39:29; Joel 2:28–29). This will further bolster people's interest in and receptivity to the things of God. Walvoord says, "Although there is no evidence that the Spirit of God will baptize believers into a spiritual unity as is true in the church today, there nevertheless will be the indwelling power and presence of the Spirit in believers in the Millennium."[68] When Jesus appeared to His disciples after He was raised from the dead, He "opened their minds" so they could understand the purpose of His death and resurrection (Luke 24:45). In the Millennium, the Holy Spirit will surely provide this same illumination to all redeemed mortals.

All of these blessings will produce an extraordinarily fertile environment for the worship of Christ by people everywhere on earth. Imagine all nations united in praise of the Messiah and guided by His truth! Picture the day when all of humankind's deepest questions about philosophy, theology, ethics, and morality are fully answered and all related issues are resolved! Today, cosmologists ponder the origin and fate of the universe almost exclusively from the viewpoint of atheistic naturalism that discounts belief in a divine Creator, but in the Millennium, all humankind will know beyond question that God created the universe and sustains it. Today philosophers and thinkers struggle to comprehend the nature of humans and our place in the world, but then, a God-centered worldview will permeate all societies on earth, reinforcing a view of humans as God's special creation, designed to live in relationship with Him. Together, these circumstances will have a purifying effect upon humankind's worship of Christ by obliterating doubt and affirming Christ's worthiness of our absolute devotion.

Israel's Worship in the Millennium

At no place on earth will worship of Christ take place with as much exuberance and ceremony as in the land of Israel. In the eschaton, the people of Israel will serve as the world's worship leaders and teachers, and Jerusalem will become the global epicenter of praise to the Messiah. Believers "from every tribe and language and people and nation" (Revelation 5:9) will travel to Israel to see Jesus and to witness His glory. As Christ's representatives, the Jews will proclaim His lordship to the world and will lead the praises of those who come to Him.

Gentiles will recognize Israel's honored status as God's chosen people, and God says in Zechariah 8:22–23 that Gentile visitors to Jerusalem will plead with individual Jews for the privilege of accompanying them into Christ's presence: "In those days ten men from all languages and nations will take firm hold of one Jew by the hem of his robe and say, 'Let us go with you, because we have heard that God is with you'" (v. 23).

Israel will celebrate at least some of the great national feasts (religious festivals) that it observed in biblical times. The Law of Moses prescribed a total of seven feasts:

Passover (Leviticus 23:5)
Unleavened Bread (Leviticus 23:6–8)
Firstfruits (Leviticus 23:9–14)
Weeks, or Pentecost (Leviticus 23:15–22)
Trumpets (Leviticus 23:23–25)
Atonement (Leviticus 23:26–32)
Tabernacles (Leviticus 23:33–44)

In ancient Israel, these feasts lasted up to several weeks, and each feast commemorated a different act of God on the nation's behalf and reminded the people of His providential role in their heritage. Whether all of Israel's feasts and holy days will be reinstituted during the Millennium is uncertain, but Scripture indicates that at least three of them will definitely be observed.

Sabbath Observance (Ezekiel 44:1–3; 46:1–3)

Sabbath keeping epitomized Judaism's worship of God more than any of Israel's religious observances. In the Millennium, Israel will observe the Sabbath each week, and Isaiah 66:23 may imply that Gentiles will also keep it: "'From one New Moon to another and from one Sabbath to another, all mankind will come and bow down before me,' says the LORD." However, this may simply mean people all over the world will worship Christ from month to month and week to week. Sabbath worship will figure prominently in the weekly administration of Messiah's temple, as pointed out in Ezekiel

46:1 by an angel who says, "'This is what the Sovereign LORD says: The gate of the inner court facing east is to be shut on the six working days, but on the Sabbath day and on the day of the New Moon it is to be opened.'" On every Sabbath, the eastern gate of the millennial temple will be opened so the priests may make offerings.

Some Bible students believe that, at the Second Coming, Christ will pass through the Eastern Gate that now stands in the Old City of Jerusalem. Although it has been sealed for hundreds of years, many believe the Eastern Gate, or "Golden Gate" as it is often referred to by Christians, will be opened for the Messiah to pass through as He comes from the Mount of Olives to Jerusalem. This belief stems from a misunderstanding of Ezekiel 44:1–3 and 46:1–3, which some readers have incorrectly understood to refer to the present Eastern Gate in the Old City of Jerusalem. However, a careful reading of these passages reveals that Ezekiel is referring to the eastern gate of the millennial temple, which will not be constructed until after the Second Coming of Christ. Randall Price adds,

> The present Golden Gate … will probably end up being torn down and reconstructed when the Third Temple is built during the Tribulation period, and the gate will certainly be leveled by the earthquake that accompanies the Messiah's advent to the Mount of Olives (Zechariah 14:4) and the topographical changes that follow (Zechariah 14:10).[69]

Passover and the Feast of Unleavened Bread

Passover was the first and most important feast instituted by God for Israel. God declared that Passover was to be observed on the fourteenth day of the first month of the Hebrew calendar (March-April on our modern calendar). It served to remind the people of their preservation by God from the death of the firstborn in Egypt and of God's deliverance of them from slavery (Exodus 12:1–14; Leviticus 23:4–5).

Passover also foreshadowed Jesus as the ultimate Passover lamb whose blood would spare all who believe in Him from eternal death. The apostle Paul called attention to this connection to Christ's substitutionary death by declaring, "Christ, our Passover lamb, has been sacrificed" (1 Corinthians 5:7). During Christ's final week the Passover feast in Jerusalem became the setting for the Last Supper and the occasion of His crucifixion (Matthew 26:17–29).

Passover was celebrated conjointly with the Feast of Unleavened Bread, which began on the day immediately following Passover and lasted for six days, and during which the Israelites ate bread made without yeast in remembrance of their haste in leaving Egypt (Exodus 12:15–20; Leviticus 23:6–8). Leaven eventually came to symbolize sin, and today Christians see in the Feast of Unleavened Bread a picture of Christ's deliverance of believers from bondage to sin so that, like the Israelites in the Exodus, they might leave behind their old ways of life.

Ezekiel 45:21–24 reveals that Israel will observe the Passover in the Millennium, in new ways and with enhanced meaning. Christ gave the Lord's Supper—otherwise called Communion—to the church as a way of remembering His death on the cross, and for millennial Israel, the Passover will also serve that purpose. At the Last Supper, Jesus said to His disciples, "'I have eagerly desired to eat this Passover with you before I suffer. For I tell you, I will not eat it again until it finds fulfillment in the kingdom of God'" (Luke 22:15–16). Jesus was telling His disciples He will partake of the Passover meal with them in His millennial kingdom as a memorial of His sacrificial death on the cross.

Ezekiel indicates there will be notable differences in how Israel will observe Passover in the Millennium from how the nation observed it in biblical times. Most conspicuously, Ezekiel makes no mention of a Passover lamb being sacrificed during it in the eschaton, and the absence of the animal will most likely serve to emphasize that Jesus is the ultimate Passover lamb who was sacrificed on the cross. Furthermore, the offerings prescribed in Ezekiel for Passover and the Feast of Unleavened Bread at the millennial temple are unique and were never required for Passover in biblical times.

The Feast of Tabernacles (Leviticus 23:33–36; Zechariah 14:16–17)

Another feast to be reinstituted in Israel during the Millennium is the Feast of Tabernacles, or "Booths" as it is translated in some Bible versions. It is sometimes called the Feast of Ingathering, because it took place immediately after the final harvest each year and was the most joyous of all the feasts. Interesting similarities exist between the Feast of Tabernacles and modern American Christians' celebration of Thanksgiving!

So significant will be the Feast of Tabernacles in the Millennium that Scripture says even Gentiles will travel from around the globe each year to participate in it: "Then the survivors from all the nations that have attacked Jerusalem will go up year after year to worship the King, the LORD Almighty, and to celebrate the Feast of Tabernacles" (Zechariah 14:16). This probably does not mean that travelling to Israel to attend the feast will be mandatory for every person on earth, but Zechariah goes on to say that any nation failing to send representatives to the feast will suffer stern discipline from the Lord.

> If any of the peoples of the earth do not go up to Jerusalem to worship the King, the LORD Almighty, they will have no rain. If the Egyptian people do not go up and take part, they will have no rain. The LORD will bring on them the plague he inflicts on the nations that do not go up to celebrate the Feast of Tabernacles. This will be the

> punishment of Egypt and the punishment of all the nations that do not go up to celebrate the Feast of Tabernacles. (Zechariah 14:17–19)

Why will Christ make the Feast Tabernacles an international event, rather than one exclusively for Israel? God instituted the Feast of Tabernacles as an annual reminder of the Israelites' desert wanderings during the Exodus when they lived in tents and makeshift shelters made of branches of trees or shrubs as they moved from place to place. The feast came in the month of Tishri, the seventh month of the Hebrew year that falls in late September and early October on our modern calendar. It lasted for seven days, during which the Israelites lived in temporary shelters constructed for the event.

Of all the national feasts of Israel, the Feast of Tabernacles will hold special significance in the Millennium because God promised Israel He will one day come and dwell with them forever. In essence, He will "tabernacle" with them:

> This is what the LORD says: "I will return to Zion and dwell in Jerusalem." (Zechariah 8:3)

> "I will put my sanctuary among them forever. My dwelling place will be with them; I will be their God, and they will be my people. Then the nations will know that I the LORD make Israel holy, when my sanctuary is among them forever." (Ezekiel 37:26–28)

These promises will be fulfilled literally in the Millennium when Christ occupies his temple in Jerusalem. Isaiah foretells that supernatural phenomena will accompany Christ's physical presence with His people reminiscent of the shekinah glory God displayed over the tabernacle of ancient Israel:

> Then the LORD will create over all of Mount Zion and over those who assemble there a cloud of smoke by day and a glow of flaming fire by night; over all the glory will be a canopy. It will be a shelter and shade from the heat of the day, and a refuge and hiding place from the storm and rain. (Isaiah 4:5–6)

The Hebrew word for shelter in verse 6 is often translated *tabernacle*, so Isaiah may be describing a dazzling supernatural tabernacle of fire and smoke projected by Christ over the entire temple area. What a spectacular sight will await visitors to Jerusalem as the Messiah's glory billows in the skies above the city by day and lights up the nights there throughout the Millennium! This will add profound meaning to the celebration of the Feast of Tabernacles each year as global pilgrims gather to celebrate God's gracious provision and the Messiah's beneficent rule. The feast will undoubtedly mark the most joyous time of year in the Holy Land, and the environs of Jerusalem will become crowded with tent cities of prefabricated shelters set up as dwelling places for international worshippers.

New Moon Observance (Numbers 10:10)

In ancient times, the Israelites determined the start of each month by the arrival of the new moon. Every first day of the month was considered holy and was commemorated with special offerings and rest from work, and Scripture foretells the New Moon observance will also take place in millennial Israel (Ezekiel 45:17; 46:1, 6). Scripture does not indicate that New Moon observance will take place among the Gentile nations.

Charles Spurgeon called Psalm 96 a "millennial anthem,"[70] because it anticipates a future time when all nations on earth will worship the Lord. It begins with the command, "Sing to the LORD a new song; sing to the LORD all the earth." John MacArthur comments, "This new song was intended for the future inauguration of the millennial rule of the Lord over the earth."[71] One day this command will be obeyed by all people of the world, and every person on earth will join together in praise to Jesus Christ as He sits enthroned in His temple in Jerusalem.

Without question, Messiah worship will define life all over world in the Millennium and will become the cross-cultural unifier of the age. A. W. Tozer called worship, "the missing jewel of the church," but in the eschaton, worship will shine with glorious brilliance on every continent and in every nation. If you have put faith in Christ for salvation, you will be there to participate in worshipping Him, and you will find praising Jesus Christ the most thrilling and satisfying experience you have ever known and will ever know.

In this chapter, we have explored details gleaned from Scripture about how believers will worship Christ in His earthly kingdom, but these are only glimpses of an activity that will prove far more glorious than we can now perceive. The real thing will be nothing short of awesome. As John Piper has expressed it, "The magnifying of Christ in the white-hot worship of all nations is the reason the world exists."[72] Yet, while worship will certainly occupy center stage in the Millennium, some aspects of millennial worship are loaded with interpretive challenges. In the following chapter, we will attempt to address and untangle some these difficulties, many of which pertain to a mystifying vision of a temple given to the prophet Ezekiel more than 2,500 years ago.

7

Ezekiel's Troublesome Temple

> "See, I will send my messenger, who will prepare the way before me. Then suddenly the Lord you are seeking will come to his temple; the messenger of the covenant, whom you desire, will come," says the LORD Almighty.
>
> —Malachi 3:1

An old maxim holds that we should never discuss politics or religion in polite company. While I can think of several ways that advice runs cross-grain with Scripture, I also acknowledge what motivates it: politics and religion often stir up boatloads of controversy. Furthermore, few topics pertaining to the Millennium provoke more disagreement among Bible students than that of religion and how it will be practiced in it. Believers have long debated numerous issues related to religion and worship in the Millennium without reaching widespread consensus.

Mark Twain said, "In religion and politics people's beliefs and convictions are in almost every case gotten at second-hand and without examination." Whether or not Twain's claim is valid, our beliefs about the Millennium, including those that pertain to religious practices during it, are far too important to base them upon hearsay, rather than rooting them in the solid ground of Scripture. If belief in a literal one-thousand-year earthly kingdom headed by Christ and centered upon worshipping Him does not bear up under close scrutiny, we should reject it. However, I have found that many objections to this belief are, themselves, the product of inadequate examination of Scripture.

Although I am convinced the premillennial view best fits the entire witness of Scripture, I recognize that embracing premillennialism will not get us out of the briar patch of disagreement because it faces many of its own interpretive challenges. In this chapter, we will attempt to resolve some of premillennialism's most controversial elements from the perspective of two guiding convictions: that Scripture is to be understood literally unless the text indicates otherwise, and that God still has a plan for Israel as His covenant people.

Ezekiel's Temple

Some of premillennialism's most disputed teachings pertain to a mysterious temple described in the Book of Ezekiel that proponents of a literal earthly kingdom believe will literally be built and that Jesus will occupy during the Millennium. Most of what the Bible reveals about this temple is found in a vision described by the prophet Ezekiel in Ezekiel 40–48, so those chapters are a frequent sparring ground for premillennialists and those who deny there will be a literal one-thousand-year reign of Christ on earth. Is Ezekiel's Temple to be understood literally or figuratively? Do religious laws and rituals connected with that temple fit better with Judaism or with Christianity? These and other questions often put premillennialists on the defensive, so we must examine them carefully.

Objection #1: Ezekiel's Temple should be understood as an allegory designed to illustrate spiritual truths, rather than as an actual physical structure.

Many interpreters deny that Ezekiel's Temple is a literal building at all and insist that it should be understood symbolically or allegorically. In their view, Ezekiel's description of a temple was intended to convey various spiritual truths in concrete terms that readers could grasp, and it does not describe an actual physical structure that did exist or ever will. Interpreting Ezekiel's account this way fails to account for the literal-sounding language of the vision and the extensive architectural and ceremonial details it includes. Therefore, most premillennialists and other students of Scripture find it more likely that Ezekiel is describing an actual building.[73]

A specific problem encountered by an allegorical approach to understanding Ezekiel's Temple is the absence of any key in Ezekiel that would identify what spiritual realities his vision is intended to portray, and this has thrown open the door to wildly subjective and often conflicting interpretations. For example, Jerome, one of the early church fathers, claimed that the wall around the temple symbolizes the church, but Pope Gregory the Great declared that the city where the temple is located represents the church. Pope Gregory identified the measuring line used by Ezekiel's angel guide in the vision as preaching.[74] Endless other elucidations have been offered, but the obvious problem is that none of them can be verified by the text. In fact, they do not arise from Scripture at all but from the minds of interpreters. Therefore, I believe we should agree with Thomas Ice, who commented, "the critics cannot tell us, based upon a textual interpretation, what Ezekiel does mean if not taken literally."[75]

Objection #2: Ezekiel's description of the topography around the temple does not match that of Jerusalem today.

Many students of prophecy who disagree with a literal interpretation of Ezekiel's Temple like to point out inconsistencies between topographical details included in Ezekiel's vision and the actual landscape in and around Jerusalem. To begin with, Ezekiel mentions "a very high mountain" from which he looks down upon the temple complex (Ezekiel 40:2), but no such mountain exists in or near Jerusalem. The Mount of Olives does rise nearby, but it is not a towering peak that would provide an observer the panoramic view of the temple complex that Ezekiel describes.

Critics also point out that the dimensions of the temple recorded by Ezekiel do not fit the Temple Mount in Jerusalem as it exists today. At present, the Temple Mount encompasses a forty-five-acre area, but Ezekiel's Temple is much larger, and its total complex will occupy 560 acres. Such a space would substantially overextend the current Temple Mount, and even the Old City of Jerusalem. Added to that, the size and dimensions of the temple complex (Ezekiel 40:5–42:20; 47:13–20; 48) and of allotments of land for the Messiah, the Prince, the twelve tribes, and others (Ezekiel 45:1–8; 47:13–48:35) are too large to fit within Israel's present natural and political boundaries.

In addition to these issues, Ezekiel 47:1–12, Joel 3:18, and Zechariah 14:8 all make reference to a river, flowing from the temple—eastward to the Dead Sea and westward to the Mediterranean—and surrounded by lush vegetation. But no river runs through Jerusalem, and one such as Ezekiel and the other biblical writers describe would displace a major portion of the current city.

All these apparent inconsistencies can be resolved easily when one considers the future geologic upheavals, including the creation of a valley running east to west, that Zechariah 14:3–4 says will occur at Christ's Second Coming (see also Isaiah 40:4, Micah 4:1, and Luke 3:5). These occurrences will no doubt create the valley and river mentioned by the prophets and will clear the way for construction of the millennial temple by altering the landscape and demolishing many existing structures that would otherwise stand in its way. Isaiah 2:2 states, "In the last days the mountain of the LORD's temple will be established as chief among the mountains; it will be raised above the hills, and all nations will stream to it." This topographical alteration will apparently take place at the same time as other massive land-altering geologic events foretold to occur just prior to the Millennium.

Objection #3: Ezekiel's mention of animal sacrifices offered in the temple (Ezekiel 43:18–27) conflicts with the New Testament's teaching that Christ was the ultimate and final sacrifice for sin.

Many nondispensationalists consider Ezekiel's account of animal sacrifices conducted in the temple to be the reef upon which belief that he is describing a literal temple founders. They argue, rather forcefully, that such sacrifices would violate the New Testament's teaching that Christ's sacrifice on the cross forever ended the need for such sacrifices. This issue definitely presents a conundrum for premillennialists, and I am aware of no explanation that answers all objections to it. However, not knowing exactly how this and other Bible difficulties can be resolved does not mean no resolution exists but that God has left some answers outside the pale of our present understanding. In Deuteronomy 29:29, Moses tells the Israelites, "The secret things belong to the LORD our God, but the things revealed belong to us and to our children forever, that we may follow all the words of this law." God has revealed in Scripture all we need to know but not nearly all we would like to know. Some matters are left secret and inexplicable in the present, but they will become clear as God's plan unfolds in the future. In the meantime, as Max Lucado perceptibly observes, "The Bible is a fence full of knotholes through which we can peek but not see the whole picture."[76]

Still, we cannot avoid the need to take a hard look at the issue of sacrifices in a millennial temple. Ezekiel's vision of a temple repeatedly states that animal sacrifices and other offerings will be made in it by an active priesthood. In Ezekiel 45:15, the angel tells of "'grain offerings, burnt offerings and fellowship offerings to make atonement for the people.'" Although the rules and procedures governing offerings and sacrifices in Ezekiel's Temple differ significantly from those given in the Law of Moses, the vision still bears a distinctly Old Testament character and feel. If Ezekiel is in fact describing a literal future temple to be employed in the Millennium, his vision raises enormously consequential and challenging theological conundrums for premillennialists. Among these, how could animal sacrifices provide atonement for sins, when the New Testament emphatically teaches that atonement was provided exclusively by Christ once for all through His death and resurrection? How could a future resumption of animal sacrifices not signal a reversal from New Testament Christianity to Old Testament Judaism?

Undeniably, the prospect of resuming animal sacrifices made in a physical temple seems to fly in the face of everything Scripture declares about Jesus's once-for-all sacrifice of Himself—particularly as set forth in the Book of Hebrews. The whole matter would appear to shut the door to a literal understanding of Ezekiel's vision and put premillennialists' backs to the wall.

While no explanation will satisfy every critic, or even answer all of my own questions regarding this enigma, three Scriptural truths do offer some light that may ultimately point the way to its resolution.

First, the Bible tells us the Millennium will be primarily for Israel, so God can keep His covenantal promises to His chosen people, and the Jews can finally fulfill their God-given mission to the world. As we saw in chapter 1, God made promises to Abraham and his descendants that have yet to be completely fulfilled. In Exodus 19:6, God told Israel, "'you will be for me a kingdom of priests and a holy nation.'" Later, He declared to them, "'I will also make you a light for the Gentiles, that you may bring my salvation to the ends of the earth'" (Isaiah 49:6). God's purpose for Israel has always been for them to become His ambassadors to the world, a missionary nation who would carry His truth to all peoples, but when Israel failed to fulfill this mandate, God set them aside "until the times of the Gentiles are fulfilled" (Luke 21:24; cf. Matthew 21:43). The times of the Gentiles is the current interval of history during which God is working more among Gentile peoples than He is among the Jews. Israel's role in God's salvation program for humanity has been temporarily placed on hold.

But God has no intention of leaving Israel on the shelf forever. In Amos 9:11, God declares, "'In that day I will restore David's fallen tent. I will repair its broken places, restore its ruins, and build it as it used to be.'" Israel, as a nation, will ultimately turn to Christ in faith and be saved. This conversion will take place during the Tribulation and will set the stage for the final realization of Israel's destiny to become a kingdom of priests who represent God to the world. We may assume that Israel's temple ministry, including animal sacrifices and offerings made in it, will demonstrate to the world the meaning of Christ's sacrifice on the cross and will proclaim God's holiness to all nations. As Lamar Eugene Cooper Sr. explains,

> The millennial kingdom will afford an opportunity for Israel to realize and practice its missionary purpose in the plan of God and practice the symbols of their covenant for the first time, in retrospect, to commemorate the redemptive work of Jesus the Messiah.[77]

David R. Reid adds,

> Then Israel, as well as the saved Gentiles of the Kingdom, will be able to see the spiritual meaning of the Old Testament sacrifices. The millennium Temple and the reinstated sacrificial system will focus attention on Jesus as Israel's Messiah and Savior of the world. In that day, Israel will finally be a light to the nations, as God originally intended.[78]

A second truth that sheds light on Ezekiel's Temple prophecy is that the Millennium is separate from the Church Age, which will end at the Rapture. Not all conditions and prohibitions that apply in the Church Age will necessarily apply then. It is therefore entirely plausible that the temple foreseen by Ezekiel and its reinstated sacrificial system will fit perfectly in the millennial age when God reinstates Israel to their original role of spiritual leadership. Although animal sacrifices are prohibited during the present Church Age, they will apparently be ordained by God as part of Israel's temple ministry during the Millennium. John Whitcomb says, "just because animal sacrifices and priests have no place in Christianity does not mean that they will have no place in Israel after the rapture of the church."[79] Charles Feinberg asks, "How is it possible to miss the teaching of Scripture that the church age is not the only or last era of God's operation in time? Because certain conditions do not obtain in our age is no guarantee that God has not indicated their presence in an age that follows ours."[80]

We should not assume this means that millennial sacrifices will have any capacity to atone for sin during the Millennium any more than they did in the past. This leads to a third truth we must recognize if we are to understand Ezekiel's prophecy, which is the millennial sacrifices themselves will have no power to save. Dispensationalists generally agree that the sacrifices will most likely serve as memorials of Christ's finished work on the cross, much as the Lord's Supper does so in our own time.

Then why, we might wonder, would the Lord's Supper not suffice as a reminder of Christ's death for citizens of the millennial kingdom? One possible answer is that the very blessedness of millennial life itself may dull the sensitivities of those who live in it to the evil of sin and to the dreadful price paid by Christ on the cross, thus making the brutality of animal sacrifices all the more instructive. Lewis Sperry Chafer and John F. Walvoord express this point well:

> In the Millennium, with its unusual spiritual blessings, the terribleness of sin and the necessity of the sacrifice of Christ may be more difficult to comprehend than in any previous dispensation. Accordingly, the sacrificial system seems to be introduced as a reminder of the necessity of the one sacrifice of Christ which alone can take away sin.[81]

Nevertheless, Ezekiel declares the sacrifices *will* somehow atone for the sins of the offerer (Ezekiel 43:20, 26; 45:15, 17, 20). Randall Price calls attention to this fact, saying, "While the memorial view has much to commend it, it does not adequately address the fact that Ezekiel … clearly says that the blood sacrifices are for 'atonement' in just the same way that Leviticus (4:20, 26, 35; 16:27; 17:11) does under the Mosaic Covenant."[82] Thoughtful believers who find this proposition troubling are completely justified in doing so.

But let's think through it. As we learned in Sunday School, animal sacrifices made under the Law of Moses in the Old Testament were able to provide atonement only on the basis of Christ's sacrifice at Calvary. As the writer of Hebrews declares, "it is impossible for the blood of bulls and goats to take away sins" (Hebrews 10:4). He clearly means that animal sacrifices have never had the capacity of providing atonement, yet God still prescribed them through Moses. Each time an Israelite brought an animal to the priests for sacrifice, payment for his sins was essentially made on credit, and the pardon he received at that moment accrued as a debt to God, which Jesus later came and paid in full with His blood. If Jesus had not died on the cross and been raised to life, every Israelite since Moses would have been left with an unpayable sin debt, and the hundreds of thousands of animal sacrifices offered on Jewish altars would have accomplished nothing.

R. H. Alexander points out:

> Never did the sacrifices and offerings deliver one from sin … Rather, the sacrifices were picture lessons and types of the Messiah's work whereby he would atone for all sin in a propitious manner through the sacrifice of his own blood once for all.[83]

Not only were the animal sacrifices picture lessons; they were also vehicles through which the atonement afforded by Christ was bestowed upon those who made them, for the Jews were required to offer them, in conjunction with a heart of faith. When we apply that insight to the future atonement presumptively provided through the millennial sacrifices, we realize that there is essentially no difference. Just as the sacrifices made under the Mosaic Law delivered provisional atonement that was ultimately secured by Jesus on the cross, so also will the sacrifices made in the future millennial temple.

We should furthermore bear in mind that Ezekiel is not the only Old Testament prophet to foresee animal sacrifices during the Millennium. Isaiah 56:6–7, 60:7, 66:18–23, Jeremiah 33:18, and Malachi 3:3–4 also indicate they will take place in that era. These additional references strongly support the prospect that Ezekiel wrote of a literal rather than a symbolic temple, and they make it far more difficult to dismiss a literal view out of hand. Seen in the light of these truths, the prospect of animal sacrifices in the Millennium becomes more conceivable.

Objection #4: The requirement of circumcision as a condition of entrance into the temple (Ezekiel 44:8) belongs to the Old Covenant rather than to the new.

In addition to animal sacrifices carried out in the millennial temple, Ezekiel's vision also foretells that the rite of circumcision will be practiced in association with it and will be required of all males who enter the temple. This difficulty can likely also be resolved when we realize that the temple laws and rituals foreseen by Ezekiel do not imply a reinstitution of Mosaic Judaism but rather the introduction of a new form of Judaism suited to the millennial age. In addition to a distinctly different floor plan for the millennial temple itself, a great many of the regulations and rituals Ezekiel associates with the temple differ significantly from those given in the Law of Moses. They are Jewish, yet they do not match the Judaism we see in the Law of Moses.[84] These differences were so alarming to the Jewish Talmudic rabbis that the Book of Ezekiel was nearly barred from the Jewish canon!

Prince Who?

Over and above these objections, another subject of controversy in Ezekiel's vision concerns the identity of the person he refers to over a dozen times simply, and somewhat enigmatically, as "the prince." No broad agreement exists among interpreters today as to who this person is, but one thing is absolutely certain: he will play a major role in the Millennium.

In Ezekiel 44:3, the Lord grants the prince sole right to sit at the eastern gate of the temple: "'The prince himself is the only one who may sit inside the gateway to eat in the presence of the LORD. He is to enter by way of the portico of the gateway and go out the same way.'" His duties include the making of offerings and officiating at the various feasts and temple ceremonies prescribed for the Israelites by the Lord. These responsibilities indicate he will be Jewish rather than Gentile and will serve as a spiritual leader of the Israelites and an administrator under authority of the Messiah. He will receive a substantial allotment of land in Palestine to the immediate west and east of the temple complex (Ezekiel 45:1–8; 48:21–22).

The ancient rabbis believed this prince would be the Messiah Himself, but this cannot be so, given obvious inconsistencies with the divine nature and personhood of Christ. The prince is not a priest and has no priestly rights, in contrast to Christ who is our High Priest (Hebrews 4:4). The prince will have sons (Ezekiel 46:16), and he must provide an offering for sins that he commits (Ezekiel 45:22). These facts confirm that he will be a flesh-and-blood human being and not the Messiah.

Many interpreters have identified the prince as David, resurrected to serve as Christ's prime minister during the Millennium. Those who hold this view often point to Ezekiel 34:24, where God declares, "'I the LORD will be their God, and my servant David will be prince among them. I the LORD have spoken.'" Likewise, the Lord states in Ezekiel 37:25, "'David my servant will be their prince forever.'" At first notice, these statements seem to verify incontrovertibly that the prince will be none other than David himself, but because the prince is capable of committing sins and of producing offspring, he cannot be David raised from the dead, because no immortalized believer can do either! Also, more than one expositor has shown that Ezekiel 37:25 very likely refers to the Messiah, rather than to the literal David.[85]

Who then is this person? Eliminating Christ and David as possibilities, and finding no further clues to his identity, we are left to conclude that he will be a Jewish believer, possibly a descendant of David, and a survivor of the Tribulation period, whom the Lord will appoint as His representative and administrator. He is "a future scion of David's dynasty who will represent the Messiah governmentally in the affairs of earth."[86] Lamar Eugene Cooper Sr. summarizes:

> The prince of Ezekiel's temple is a godly representative of the messianic King. He will sit in the gate, commune with God, and serve as a guarantor of mercy, justice, and righteousness. He will be the perfect spiritual-administrative leader of the new kingdom.[87]

Orthodox Jews today accept that Ezekiel foretells a time when the Messiah will come and establish the kingdom of Zion on the earth and that a grand new temple will serve as the religious centerpiece of that kingdom. Although the answers provided in this chapter may not settle all the objections I have pointed out, I believe they do offer plausible explanations for serious Bible students' concerns over Ezekiel's Temple and its evident place in the Millennium.

One of the most convincing evidences that Ezekiel describes a literal millennial temple is the fact that Isaiah, Joel, and Haggai also make reference to a millennial temple (Isaiah 2:3; 60:13; Joel 3:18; Haggai 2:7, 9). Using a normal, grammatical-historical method of interpretation, there is simply no getting around it: a grand and glorious temple will exist in Jerusalem, astir with religious activity, throughout the coming Millennium.

8

The Eternal State

> And I heard a loud voice from the throne saying, "Now the dwelling of God is with men, and he will live with them. They will be his people, and God himself will be with them and be their God. He will wipe every tear from their eyes. There will be no more death or mourning or crying or pain, for the old order of things has passed away."
>
> —Revelation 21:3–4

For most of my life, I have lived near the Atlantic Ocean. I remember my very first trip to the beach, taken when I was five years old. Our family had just moved from Alabama to northern Florida near Fernandina Beach. While my dad attended to things at our new home, my mother and grandmother drove me to the seashore for a brief visit. I will never forget catching sight of the vast, brooding Atlantic spread out before me. It seemed the whole world came to an abrupt end where land met water. The view filled me with a mixture of sensations, including awe and wonder. "How far does it go?" I asked, staring at the horizon. My mother and grandmother explained that the ocean stretched on for thousands of miles, but I could not wrap my young mind around the sheer magnitude of what my eyes were beholding, and that made me a little afraid.

In a manner of speaking, the Millennium ends at the seashore. Scripture reveals that, at the close of the Millennium, many familiar things in life will vanish forever. Perhaps even time itself will end at that point. The Bible provides only sparse glimpses of life beyond the Millennium, so details are extremely limited. When we try to imagine what eternity will be like, our heads fill with questions: How will my life in eternity be different from what it is now? Will I be content? Should I fear it? Such questions are normal responses to anything unknown and mysterious, but Scripture reveals enough about our existence in eternity to assure us God has great things in store for His people, and we have no cause for worry.

Interpreters generally use the terms "eternal state" and "final state" to denote the postmillennial destiny of God's people and His creation. Jesus referred to it as either "eternal punishment" or "eternal life," depending upon whether or not a person is born again (Matthew 25:46). For the purposes of this book, our interest in the eternal state pertains only to how it relates to what God begins during the Millennium and how He brings it to completion. The Millennium and the eternal state should not be understood as two separate ages but as two parts of the same era of human history.

Scripture's first mention of the eternal state is found in Isaiah 65:17, in which God says, "Behold, I will create new heavens and a new earth. The former things will not be remembered, nor will they come to mind." This new creation pertains to the eternal state, rather than to the Millennium. In the New Testament, Peter refers to Isaiah's prophecy when he writes in 2 Peter 3:13, "But in keeping with his promise we are looking forward to a new heaven and a new earth, the home of righteousness." Then, in Revelation 21:1–22:6, the apostle John describes what he saw of that new world in a vision given to him by God: "Then I saw a new heaven and a new earth, for the first heaven and the first earth had passed away" (21:1). Using a historical-grammatical method of interpreting those texts, we find no reason why we should not take literally the promise they contain of a new world and universe.

Students of Scripture hold differing opinions on whether the new heavens and new earth will be actual replacements of the present heavens and earth, or the current ones made like new through restoration.[88] An analysis of the merits of each view lies outside the scope of this book, but regardless of which interpretation is correct, we can be certain that our future eternal home and the things we experience in it will be more wonderful than anything in our wildest dreams.

When astronomers encounter something in the cosmos so bizarre that it defies comprehension, they call it a "singularity." (Think black holes.) For theologians, the eternal state qualifies as a kind of singularity because of how dramatically it differs from our present existence, including its infinite duration. The late astronomer Isaac Asimov once noted, "Throughout history, men have tended to avoid the concept of endlessness in either space or time as something impossible to grasp and understand and therefore something that cannot easily be worked with or reasoned about."[89] The eternal state will be characterized not only by endlessness but also by absolute righteousness. Earth will exist, but it will be an earth that is dramatically different from the earth on which we now live and to which all of our experiences are tied. God will be there, and we will worship Him but not in temples or church buildings. Life will be virtually unrecognizable compared to life as we know it now—and infinitely grander!

Interpreters wrangle over how literally the Bible's descriptions of the new heavens and new earth should be taken, but most of these accounts contain no indicators that they should be understood as anything but literal, and nonliteral interpretations of them are pointless when we consider God's unlimited capabilities. For example, in the Book of Revelation, the apostle John says oceans will be absent in the new earth (21:1). We know earth's oceans play an integral role in our planet's climate and weather patterns, so some interpreters scoff at the idea that oceans will not exist in the new earth, but can God not alter geophysical laws that will govern weather conditions in the future earth? In fact, it seems most likely He will do so! "He who was seated on the throne said, 'I am making *everything* new'" (21:5). We should expect that "everything" may very well include the natural laws under which our universe exists and by which it operates.

John also implies no sun or moon will exist in the new heavens. The sun is essential to life in our present world for many reasons, not the least of which is its provision of light. But John says God's own glory will provide ample light in the new world (Revelation 21:23). John adds, "there will be no night there" (21:25). Nighttime and darkness will give way to eternal daylight that radiates from God Himself. All these revelations challenge us to simply take God at His word. By faith, we trust God will make the new earth suitable for life to exist, and we do not need for Him to explain to us how He will do it, any more than we need for Him to describe how He raised dead people to life in the miracle stories of the Bible. God is God, and absolutely nothing is impossible for Him.

In Revelation 21:1–22:6, the apostle John describes seeing the "the Holy City, the New Jerusalem" in a vision given to him by God. Christians widely believe John's vision was of heaven itself, and the features he describes are things many believers expect to see in heaven, including gates of pearl and streets of gold. Some interpreters insist the city should be taken as symbolical rather than literal, on the presumption that its enormous size (1,800 miles square and high by some estimates) exceeds the bounds of reason if taken literally.[90] However, the detail with which John describes the city seems pointless if it is nonliteral. Similar to Ezekiel's vision of the temple, recorded in Ezekiel 40–48, an angel guides John and takes precise measurements of the city, and interpreters who believe the vision is nonliteral or allegorical are at a loss to explain the meaning of these details. Furthermore, nothing in John's language suggests anything but a literal interpretation is intended.

John presents this gleaming city as the centerpiece of the new earth and the home of all God's people in the eternal state. In John's vision, the city is seen "coming down out of heaven from God" (Revelation 21:2). The city will shine with the light of God the Father and of Christ, both of whom will sit enthroned within it (22:1, 3), and no trace of evil or sin will ever pollute it.

Although we may crave to discover everything there is to know about the eternal state, the Bible offers very little more information about it other than the few details we have mentioned here. Nevertheless, a great deal of insight can be gleaned from Scripture as to what the eternal state will accomplish in God's eternal plan. By considering these outcomes, we can begin to appreciate the essential role the eternal state plays in the grand sweep of redemptive history.

The Curse Repealed Entirely

As we have seen earlier in this book, during the Millennium, God will begin to lift the curse He pronounced upon creation when Adam and Eve sinned in Eden. As we saw in chapter 3, this partial removal of the curse will probably apply only to the land of Israel at first. But, in the eternal state, God will lift the curse entirely from all His creation. John Walvoord explains:

> In the millennial scene, there is a lifting of the curse upon the earth, but not a total deliverance from the world's travail brought in by sin, for in the Millennium, it is still possible for a 'sinner' to be 'accursed' (Isa. 65:20) with resulting physical death. In the new heaven and the new earth, there will be no curse at all and no possibility or need of such divine punishment.[91]

In Romans 8, the apostle Paul encourages believers to set our hope upon the future glory we will share with God when "the creation itself will be liberated from its bondage to decay and brought into the glorious freedom of the children of God" (8:21). He notes that "the whole creation has been groaning as in the pains of childbirth right up to the present time" (8:22). In other words, the natural world itself longs for the curse to be lifted. This promise will be brought to fruition in the new heavens and earth. Of that future time, the apostle John declares triumphantly, "No longer will there be any curse" (Revelation 22:3). God's removal of the curse will impact every aspect of life in the new earth. His perfecting of the natural world will have been limited to Palestine during the Millennium, but in the eternal state, it will extend to every corner of the globe. Every trace of the curse will vanish, including destructive storms and earthquakes, droughts and famine, sickness and disease, and predation in nature. Presumably, men and women will regain the equality and harmony Adam and Eve enjoyed together before they forfeited it because of sin. Every blessing God revoked when human beings fell from Him will be reinstated fully and forever, with brand-new blessings added in!

In Revelation 21:4, John says, "[God] will wipe every tear from their eyes. There will be no more death or mourning or crying or pain, for the old order of things has passed away." By "the old order of things," John means all of the debilitating physical, psychological, and spiritual effects of the curse that plague our existence in this present world. In reference to what John says in that verse, Kendall H. Easley states, "The last thought could also be translated, 'The former things are gone.' No greater statement of the end of one kind of existence and the beginning of a new one can be found in Scripture."[92]

Evil and Unrighteousness Banished

John writes of the New Jerusalem, saying, "Nothing impure will ever enter it, nor will anyone who does what is shameful or deceitful, but only those whose names are written in the Lamb's book of life" (Revelation 21:27). Sin, and those who commit it, will not be found anyplace in universe. As we have explained earlier in this book, mortal human beings will live on earth during the Millennium, and they will possess a sin nature. Although commission of sin by human beings will decrease sharply because of Satan's absence and Christ's firm rule, sin will nonetheless exist to some extent in the Millennium. But, in the eternal state, only glorified, immortal believers will live on earth, and their sin natures will have been purged from them, so sin will cease to exist entirely.

In the eternal state, God will erase the very memory of evil from our minds. In Isaiah 65:17, God says, "'Behold, I will create new heavens and a new earth. The former things will not be remembered, nor will they come to mind.'" Because of the pervasiveness of sin and suffering in our present world, recollections of this life would almost certainly call to mind things that bring us pain and sadness, and God will simply not permit that to happen, and so we will have no recollection of sin or of anything unpleasant or disturbing related to the fallen world in which we now live. In eternity, it will seem as though evil never existed! Thus, our lives will be characterized by absolute righteousness, perfect peace, and endless joy.

God the Father Acknowledged as Supreme

During the Millennium, God the Father will cause Christ to be exalted as King of kings, and as we discovered in chapter 4, this will fulfill the Father's many promises to glorify Jesus by giving Him a kingdom and bringing "all things in heaven and on earth together under one head, even Christ" (Ephesians 1:10). Then, when the

Millennium has ended, as we have already seen, Jesus will hand over His kingdom to God the Father, and the Father will be exalted as supreme (1 Corinthians 15:24–28). Although God intends for all of creation, including the human race, to glorify Christ at the present time, the ultimate purpose—the sine qua non—of everything everywhere is the acknowledgment of the Father as supreme.

Immediately after the close of the apostolic era, theologians began wrestling with the question of how Jesus will reign forever, as Scripture repeatedly affirms He will (Isaiah 9:6–7; Daniel 2:44–45; Luke 1:32–33; 2 Peter 1:11; Revelation 1:6; 11:15), yet at some point He will hand over the kingdom to God the Father. In the second century AD, a Christian heresy called Subordinationism arose, which taught that God the Son and God the Holy Spirit are not divine to the same extent as God the Father is. It held that the Son and the Spirit are inferior to the Father in both nature and being. While such a notion is blatantly unbiblical, what are we to make of this "transfer of power" that will take place at the outset of the eternal state?

It is helpful to keep in mind that the New Testament speaks of Christ's reign in two different ways. He reigns as God, and He also reigns as Messiah, the Savior of those who put their trust in Him. Perhaps Paul is telling us in 1 Corinthians 15:24–28 that Christ's reign as Messiah during the Millennium will give way to His reigning exclusively as the Son of God throughout eternity, who is, along with the Holy Spirit, in every way equal to the Father with respect to His deity.[93]

God the Father Reunited with His People

Before sin made its entrance into the world in the Garden of Eden, God the Father related to Adam and Eve directly, with no need for a go-between to relay messages back and forth. The Father communicated with them firsthand and in real time, and Adam and his wife enjoyed intimate fellowship with Him. But when Adam and Eve listened to the serpent and violated God's command by eating the fruit of the Tree of the Knowledge of Good and Evil, this intimacy with God was lost. A chasm opened up between humankind and God. Not only did their sin destroy their relationship with God, but it also rendered His firsthand contact with them impossible.

Ever since that tragic event, which theologians refer to as the Fall of humankind, the Father has related to His people and ruled over them indirectly through agents of His own choosing. In the Old Testament, God first used Moses and then the Levitical priests as His representatives before people. Today, Christ serves as our Great High Priest (Hebrews 4:14), and He intercedes for us before the Father, as does also the Holy Spirit (Romans 8:26–27, 34). Even during the Millennium, God the Father will not relate to or rule over mortal human beings directly but will do so through Christ as His intermediary. Theologians often describe this arrangement as the "mediatorial kingdom,"[94] of which Christ's millennial kingdom will be a part. Alva McCain says, "The Mediatorial Kingdom of our Lord will constitute the glorious consummating era of the first order of things and will serve as the divine bridge between the temporal order and the eternal order."[95]

When the Millennium gives way to the eternal state, the mediatorial kingdom will end, and God the Father will forever afterward interact directly with His people. This reunion of God and the human race is emphasized by the repeated use of the word "with" in God's declaration at the outset of the eternal state: "And I heard a loud voice from the throne saying, 'Now the dwelling of God is *with* men, and he will live *with* them. They will be his people, and God himself will be *with* them and be their God'" (Revelation 21:3). Only redeemed believers will inhabit the eternal kingdom, and we will enjoy direct fellowship with the Father. He will speak to us face-to-face, and vice versa, and never again will it be necessary for the Son or the Holy Spirit to intercede before the Father on our behalf. In the *Jamieson, Fausset, and Brown Commentary*, Robert

Jamieson says, "God shall then come into direct connection with the earth, instead of mediatorially, when Christ shall have fully and finally removed everything that severs asunder the holy God and a sinful earth."[96] What an unimaginably wonderful day that will be!

Continuation and Expansion of Millennial Blessings

In the eternal state, God will carry on forever the blessings He will initiate during the Millennium. As we have said, it is important for us not to think of the Millennium and the eternal state as disconnected from one another. Instead, we should view the Millennium as the opening act of the eternal state. While it is true that certain aspects of the Millennium will not carry over into the eternal state, such as Christ conquering nations and disciplining those who disobey Him, some aspects of life in the Millennium will foreshadow life in eternity. Also, the millennial blessings God promised to Israel, including the restoration of the natural world, will be expanded to include the entire earth.

Envision the Millennium as stage one of the eternal state. For example, we have already seen that, in the Millennium, God will fulfill all of the covenantal promises He made to Abraham, to David, and to the Jewish people. These promises include Israel's possession of the Promised Land, Christ's kingship over Israel, and the reign of resurrected believers in God's kingdom. In each case, God said He will keep His promise eternally, and therefore His promises will not be limited to the millennial kingdom but will carry on forever (Deuteronomy 4:40; Revelation 11:15; 22:5).

God also promised that, in the Millennium, physical death will be radically curtailed within Israel, but in the eternal state, death will be eliminated throughout the entire world (Revelation 21:4). Other promises God made to Israel, such as causing Israel's land to become abundantly fruitful, will presumably come true throughout the new earth. Although specific information about the eternal state is limited in Scripture, one thing is certain: the new heavens and earth will be absolutely flawless in every way—the perfect home for God's glorified people throughout eternity!

Christian author Steven D. Matthewson says, "Life on the new earth in the new Jerusalem is the life you have always wanted—without tears, death, mourning, crying, and pain that make life miserable."[97] God has blessed believers with a glimpse of the glorious eternity in which we will live following the Millennium, and we are indeed grateful for what He has revealed to us in Scripture. Even so, when we study what the Bible says about it, we become like children gathered at the seashore, awestruck by the ocean's immensity. Billy Graham tells of an American Indian who visited the ocean for the first time and was awestruck at the sight. The old Indian asked for someone to fetch a quart jar, which he then dipped into the waves to fill it with seawater. When a bystander asked what he planned to do with the water, he said he would take the jar back to his people who had never seen the Great Water, so they could know what it is like.[98] The sum of what we know about the eternal state is like water in a quart jar, but that is enough.

What would we do with more knowledge of eternity if we had it? We might find such knowledge confusing or even frightening because it is utterly foreign to our experience. Or perhaps we would become so enamored with what we discovered that we would daydream about the future and fail to serve Jesus in the present. Whatever the case, our wisest course is to take the glimpses of eternity that God has provided to us and do with them what children do with seashells they gather at the beach: take them home and enjoy them as treasured keepsakes. That way, those glimpses can continually remind us of the blessed future awaiting us beyond the far horizon.

9

When the Perfect Comes

> You have made known to me the path of life; you will fill me with joy in your presence, with eternal pleasures at your right hand.
>
> —Psalm 16:11

"The greatest adventure we could ever imagine awaits us in the coming kingdom of Christ."[99] Those words by Canadian author Grant R. Jeffrey capture the thrilling truths presented in this book. Nineteenth-century Bible scholar Nathaniel West declared, "Next to the eternal state, the millennial blessedness of God's people on earth, and of the nations, is the one high point in all prophecy, from Moses to John, the bright, broad tableland of all eschatology."[100] If you are a believer in Christ, you can look forward to someday filling your lungs with the fresh, pure air of that broad tableland when you return to earth with Him at His Second Coming.

One of the many benefits of studying what the Bible reveals about the Millennium and the eternal state is the irrepressibly positive outlook on life that it produces in you, because you know eternity for believers will bring joy, peace, and contentment on a scale that will far exceed anything we can imagine now. How could any follower of Christ not overflow with anticipation when they discover that all of the best things in this life are mere foretastes of what we will enjoy in eternity!

When God surveyed the universe at the end of the creation week, He "saw all that he had made, and it was very good" (Genesis 1:31). God brought the universe into existence in a state of absolute perfection, and the natural world was innately good, as also were human beings, the foundational institutions of marriage and the home, the gift of work, and the quality of life itself. But, because of humankind's fall and God's consequent curse upon creation, today nearly nothing you and I encounter in the world retains the goodness that characterized it originally. Nevertheless, Scripture assures us that God will one day restore His creation and make it perfect once again. Eden is scheduled for a comeback! Virtually everything we value and enjoy in this world will become innately better in Christ's millennial kingdom, and all of it will regain its original perfection in the new heavens and new earth that come afterward. No vision of the future could spark more optimism than that!

The ancient Greek philosopher Plato believed tangible objects in the world, and intangible qualities such as beauty and goodness, have a corresponding ideal form of themselves existing in some otherworldly realm and that those prototypical forms are pure and flawless. For Plato, the earthly versions of these things—the ones we experience and interact with—are imperfect copies of those ideal forms.[101] Of course, Plato was a pagan who did not know or believe God's truth, but some students of theology see similarity between Plato's theory of the forms and the contrast Scripture describes between the curse-caused defects of our world and the perfections of heaven. Christianity certainly does affirm that you and I live in a less than ideal world, and neither we ourselves nor much of anything we encounter in our lifetimes can rightly be called perfect. However, the Bible assures us that everything God's people encounter in eternity will be utterly faultless and good. We can therefore concede that Plato's thinking bore a vague and inadvertent resemblance to what

Scripture says about the way things actually are. As the old saw goes, "Even a blind squirrel finds a nut once in a while!"

So, how does that connect with life in the Millennium? When a child of God arrives in Christ's eternal kingdom, he or she will enter a realm in which things exist that they also encountered in this present world; only there, many of those things will have been made perfect once again. As a nineteenth-century minister once wrote, "All the splendors of this world which we now inhabit are only faint beams of the glory yet to be revealed."[102] What sorts of splendors are we talking about? Let's consider a few of the most prominent ones.

Eternally Fulfilling Relationships

For starters, all of our relationships in Christ's kingdom will be ideal. As deeply satisfying as love and friendship are to us in our present world, imagine how much more so they will become in eternity! The pleasure that you receive now from enjoying a cup of coffee with a friend, or walking hand in hand with your spouse in a park on a warm spring day, or tossing a ball with your grandchild will increase exponentially in the relationships you enjoy with other believers in Christ's kingdom. At the same time, relationship spoilers such as jealously, insecurity, impatience, and selfishness will not affect our connections with others as they do now, and no relationship between believers in eternity will end—ever.

Eternal Enjoyment of Beauty

Our enjoyment of all things beautiful will also find ultimate fulfillment in heaven, and then in the Millennium and eternal state. God endowed human beings with an aesthetic awareness that instinctively attracts us to beauty, as moths are drawn to flame. This awareness enables us to take pleasure in the world's natural beauty and in the arts, and it motivates us to decorate our homes and workplaces. We possess this capacity to recognize and value that which is beautiful precisely because our Creator is the essence of beauty. As pastor John Piper describes it, God's glory is "the infinite beauty and greatness of his manifold perfections."[103] And because God made us for Himself, something deep within us is drawn to that which reminds us of Him.

Believers have recognized this correlation between our love of beauty and our need of God for centuries. In the thirteenth century, Thomas Aquinas said, "The beauty of creatures is nothing other than the image of the divine beauty in which things participate."[104] Centuries later, Jonathan Edwards expressed the same idea when he wrote that "God … is the foundation and fountain of all being and all beauty."[105] This means that your longing for beauty leads you upon a pursuit that can be satisfied only by God and ultimately by enjoying His unveiled presence in eternity. In the meantime, when your eye is drawn to a picturesque landscape, or you find yourself enjoying a piece of good music, you are feeling the nudge of a built-in homing beacon that God hard wired into you to steer you toward Himself.

Steven D. Matthewson notes that we all bear "the empty print and trace" of authentic joy and happiness that the human race lost by rebelling against God, and he quotes Blaise Pascal, who argues that most efforts to satisfy this void in our lives do not work "since this infinite Abyss can be filled only with an infinite and immutable object; in other words by God himself."[106] C. S. Lewis expressed the character and depth of our longing when he wrote, "We do not want merely to *see* beauty … We want something else which can hardly be put into words—to be united with the beauty we see, to pass into it, to receive it into ourselves, to bathe in it, to become part of it."[107] In other words, we crave to be where God is, to experience Him with all of our senses, and to live with Him forever, and no other attachment or relationship can fulfill that longing. It is, as Lewis described it, "a desire which no natural happiness can satisfy."[108] This means that, until our earthly sojourn is over and our union with God is fully consummated in eternity, our deepest need will remain unmet and our innermost yearning will go unfulfilled.

In his book *The Reason for God*, Timothy Keller contends that our love of beauty testifies of God's existence, because beauty evokes in us a hunger that can be satisfied only by God, and he reasons that it is impossible to crave that which does not exist.[109] Lewis made the same point, reasoning that our desire for paradise is "a pretty good indication that such a thing exists and that some men will [live in it]."[110] In Psalm 27:4, this "God craving" peaks out of David's heart as he declares his yearning to gaze upon the Lord's beauty all the days of his life. In heaven, and on earth in the Millennium and the eternal state, when we stand astonished at the sight of Christ seated "on his throne in heavenly glory" (Matthew 25:31), His divine beauty will fulfill these yearnings in us completely and forevermore.

Home Forever

"There's no place like home." Who could watch the climactic scene in the movie *The Wizard of Oz* and not identify with Dorothy when she closed her eyes, clicked her heels together three times, and repeated those words over and over? Few words in any language evoke emotions as heartfelt and profound in us as the word "home." For believers in Christ, virtually no other word so keenly embodies our expectations of what spending eternity with our Lord will be like.

Warsan Shire, a Somali poet who lives in England, put her finger squarely upon what I am saying here when she wrote, "Maybe home is somewhere I'm going and never have been before."[111] For believers in Christ, home is ultimately found in the presence of God Himself, and none of us is going to feel fully at home until we see His face (Revelation 22:4). My mother lived with us for ten years before she succumbed to congestive heart failure, and shortly before she died, she sensed her departure was near. A few days before she passed away, she said to me, "I think I'm going home soon." Mom was a committed Christian, and she knew she would soon be with Jesus. For believers, death is the ultimate homecoming, and when we arrive in Christ's eternal kingdom, we will know we have arrived home at last.

Let's face it: we humans are notorious malcontents who are prone to incessant dissatisfaction. Rarely, if ever, do we consider everything in our lives to be just right. In some respects, these moods are pangs of our spiritual homesickness. Augustine, the early church father, arrived at this conclusion in the fourth century and famously confessed to God, "Thou hast made us for thyself, O Lord, and our heart is restless until it finds its rest in thee." Simply put, we wanna go home! Long before Augustine, Solomon noted that God "has also set eternity in the hearts of men; yet they cannot fathom what God has done from beginning to end" (Ecclesiastes 3:11). Solomon seemed to be saying that God implanted in each of us an awareness of our soul's own eternal existence and that He made us to crave Himself, whether or not each of us realizes it is God whom we yearn for.

Perhaps you were blessed with a loving and happy home while growing up, or maybe your experience of home was anything but joyful. Whatever the case, a pleasant home is something we all desire on an instinctual level, and nothing can compensate for the lack of it. For believers in Christ, home is not a place but a person, and if you are born again, you will one day arrive at home to live with Jesus forever. English theologian John Bate wrote, "Everything is restless until it comes home." In Christ's eternal kingdom, every one of us who has placed faith in Christ will find that his deep-seated homesickness has been cured forever.

Perfect Holiness

If you are a Christian, you live in a relentless tug-of-war between your redeemed mind and your unredeemed flesh. You want to live like Jesus, but you do not find an obedient lifestyle easy to maintain on a day-to-day basis because you still possess a sin nature that continually seeks gratification of fleshly desires (see Galatians 5:17). As theologian Edward Oakes has said, we are "born into a world where rebellion against God has already taken place and the drift of it sweeps us along."[112]

Bible teacher and author Warren Wiersbe points out that the reason our sin nature remains with us after our conversion to Christ is that our souls have been redeemed, but our bodies have not.[113] In Romans 8:23, Paul says, "we ourselves, who have the firstfruits of the Spirit, groan inwardly as we wait eagerly for our adoption as sons, the redemption of our bodies." If believers on earth are presently waiting for bodily redemption, it obviously has not yet occurred, but it will take place the moment we meet Christ. At that moment, we will be set free from our sin nature and delivered from our lifelong battle with temptation. The Greek word that is translated "redeem" in our English Bibles literally means "to set free." How our hearts ache for that moment of triumph! For now though, our struggle goes on.

As followers of Jesus, we can readily identify with the apostle Paul's frustrations over his own inability to make a permanent break with sin, which he openly acknowledges in Romans 7. Paul admits, "I know that nothing good lives in me, that is, in my sinful nature. For I have the desire to do what is good, but I cannot carry it out" (Romans 7:18). Brother Paul, we all feel your pain! Like him, no matter how high a level of spiritual maturity we may attain, we can never live entirely sin-free in this life. But, praise God, in heaven and in Christ's eternal kingdom on earth, we will at last be purged of our sinful inclinations and made holy—not only in terms of our position in Christ but in actual practice.

Like Paul, we know in our heads what God expects of us, but we cannot fully live up to those expectations. Someday, though, God will rescue us from "this body of death" (Romans 7:24) in which we now live, and He will enable us to throw off sin forever. Wiersbe notes, "When Christ finally imprisons Satan, He will deliver the entire creation from this bondage, and all nature will enjoy with us 'the glorious freedom of the children of God' (Romans 8:21)."[114] What wonderful news it is that our lifelong battle with temptation is destined to be won at that future moment when God makes each of us like Jesus!

Perhaps you have always associated the blessings we are describing in this chapter exclusively with heaven, but you will experience them just the same when you return to earth with Christ and live in His kingdom. In the eternal state, you will live in the Father's presence and serve Him alongside countless fellow believers and angels in a world of unimaginable purity, beauty, and glory. You will not recall anything ungodly or evil, and you will have no recollection of sadness, loneliness, or anxiety, because God will mercifully purge all such memories from your mind.

We have seen in this book that, from Genesis to Revelation, Scripture is filled with references to Christ's eternal kingdom. All of this attention given to the eschaton signifies that a fantastic and wonderful future awaits all of God's people, because someday His kingdom will become our eternal home. In the meantime, studying the Bible's many references to that magnificent era offers us enticing insights into the glorious eternity to come. As Nathaniel West observes, "Nothing can be of greater interest to a student of God's Word than to watch the development of the 1000 years" [115] in the Bible.

Furthermore, as we begin to understand the nature of God's future kingdom and realize what a central place it holds in Scripture, we become enabled to grasp the big picture of God's eternal plan. Grant R. Jeffrey says, "The prophecies about the coming kingdom provide the key to the true understanding of the Scriptures and God's plan for redeeming humanity from the curse of sin."[116] Such comprehension is impossible without an understanding of the role of Christ's millennial kingdom in His blueprint for the future.

In Orlando, Florida, Walt Disney World offers visitors more than forty-five individual rides and attractions that span an assortment of themes ranging from the magical to the futuristic, but only one—the Carousel of Progress—can boast of having been ridden by Walt Disney himself. As part of the original park that opened in Orlando in 1971, the Carousel of Progress ranks among the oldest rides in the Magic Kingdom. It celebrates how past innovations in consumer products have improved humankind's quality of life, and it predicts how advances in technology that are yet to come will shape our future. Visitors on the ride hear the carousel's cheery theme song, "There's a Great Big Beautiful Tomorrow."[117] The song's prediction is true but not because of better gadgets. It's true because Jesus is coming back!

Scripture tells us God has planned a truly bright and beautiful tomorrow for every person who places faith in Him, a real-life never-never land where believers will live happily throughout eternity. In the words of the Westminster Shorter Catechism, "Man's chief end is to glorify God, and to enjoy him forever."[118] For all the reasons we have pointed out in this chapter, the Millennium and eternity will outshine anything human beings can ever produce by means of technological improvements, political achievement, or social action.

The word *utopia* was coined by Sir Thomas More for his famous sixteenth-century novel that bears that title. Surprisingly, it means "no place," presumably because, for More, it represented a perfect ideal that he believed could never be realized and that exists only in our imaginations. Though human beings can never create a perfect world independent of God, many have tried. For thousands of years, visionaries and idealists of every stripe have promoted their own brands of utopia. Political science professor Lyman Tower Sargent notes, "There are socialist, capitalist, monarchical, democratic, anarchist, ecological, feminist, patriarchal, egalitarian, hierarchical, racist, left-wing, right-wing, reformist, free love, nuclear family, extended family, gay, lesbian, and many more utopias."[119] But none of them work! They amount to nothing more than rearranging deck chairs on the *Titanic*, because they are all humanistic, unbiblical, and doomed to failure.

More than any other benefit that comes from awareness of the eternity God has in store for His people is how it equips us to lead more God-honoring lives today. We find renewed motivation to make a difference in the present world by sharing the good news of Christ with all who will receive it. We also develop a clearer and more biblical understanding of life after death and a resilient hope for the future that can sustain us through all of this life's troubles and sorrows. As the apostle Paul declared, "We have this hope as an anchor for the soul, firm and secure" (Hebrews 6:19).

For believers in Christ, the future of our world amounts to a real-life cliff-hanger. Does God keep His promises to give His chosen people a perpetual homeland? Does God make good on His word to give Christ an earthly kingdom? Will every knee bow to Christ and every tongue confess that He is Lord? Will believers reign with Christ on earth? The answers to all of these burning questions lie in the Millennium! And because those answers will all be yes, they portend good news—the very best possible news—for God's people today.

In the 1930s, Gabriel Heater hosted a nightly news show on the radio. Although Heater was broadcasting in the midst of the Great Depression, with war clouds building over Europe and then the Pacific, he always started his newscast with "Ah yes, friends, there's good news tonight." For believers in Christ, no matter how gloomy the headlines and newscasts may sound, the Bible's preview of our future conveys assurance of good news to come. J. I. Packer points out to us the bottom line of all we have seen in this book by saying, "So the life of heavenly glory is a compound of seeing God in and through Christ and being loved by the Father and the Son, of rest and work, of praise and worship, and of fellowship with the Lamb and the saints. The hearts of those in heaven say, I want this to go on forever. And it will. There can be no better news than this."[120]

It will, indeed, go on forever, on a new earth born from the ashes of disaster toward which human sin is inexorably hurtling this planet, and that is the reason why knowing Christ and living for Him today is worth it all.

Bibliography

Alcorn, Randy. *Heaven: Gods Answers for Your Every Need.* Carol Stream, Illinois: Tyndale House, 2008.

Alexander, R. H. *The Expositor's Bible Commentary—Isaiah—Ezekiel: With the New International Version of the Holy Bible.* Edited by Frank E. Gaebelein. Vol. 6. Grand Rapids: Zondervan Pub. House, 1986.

Alperin, Michele. "Next Year in Jerusalem." My Jewish Learning. Accessed December 01, 2018. https://www.myjewishlearning.com/article/next-year-in-jerusalem/.

Anderson, David A. "The Aggregate Burden of Crime." *SpringerLink.* January 31, 1999. Accessed May 9, 2015. http://dx.doi.org/10.2139/ssrn.147911.

Asimov, Isaac. *The Universe: From Flat Earth to Quasar.* New York: Avon, 1966.

Benware, Paul N. *Understanding End Times Prophecy: A Comprehensive Approach.* Chicago: Moody Publishers, 2006.

Blaising, Craig A., Carmen Hardin, and Thomas C. Oden. *Ancient Christian Commentary on Scripture,* vol. 13. Downers Grove, IL: InterVarsity Press, 2008.

Boa, Kenneth, and Robert M. Bowman Jr. *Sense and Nonsense about Heaven and Hell.* Grand Rapids: Zondervan, 2007.

Bonar, Horatius. "The Jew." *Quarterly Journal of Prophecy* 23 (July 1870): 215.

Brown, Colin. *The New International Dictionary of New Testament Theology: Translated, With Additions and Revisions, from the German*. Vol. 3. Grand Rapids, MI: Zondervan, 1978.

Cairns, Alan. *Dictionary of Theological Terms*. Greenville, SC: Ambassador Emerald International, 2002.

Chafer, Lewis Sperry, and John F. Walvoord. *Major Bible Themes: 52 Vital Doctrines of the Scripture Simplified and Explained*. Revised ed. Grand Rapids, MI: Zondervan, 1974.

Chafer, Lewis Sperry. *Systematic Theology*. Vol. 4. Grand Rapids, MI: Kregel Publications, 1993.

_____. "Come Thou Fount of Every Blessing." Wikipedia. July 11, 2019. Accessed July 15, 2019. https://en.wikipedia.org/wiki/Come_Thou_Fount_of_Every_Blessing.

Cooper, Lamar Eugene. *The New American Commentary: An Exegetical and Theological Exposition of Holy Scripture: NIV Text*. Vol. 17. Nashville, TN: B & H Pub. Group, 1994.

Dillow, Th D. Joseph. *Final Destiny: The Future Reign of the Servant Kings*. Conroe, TX: Grace Theology Press, 2018.

Durant, Will, and Ariel Durant. *Lessons of History*. New York: Simon & Schuster, 2010.

Easley, Kendell, and Max Anders. *Holman New Testament Commentary—Revelation*. Vol. 12. Nashville, TN. B & H Publishing Group, 2014.

Edersheim, Alfred. *The Temple: Its Ministry and Services*. Peabody, MA: Hendrickson, 1995.

Edworthy, Niall, Petra Cramsie, and Emily Faccini. *The Optimist's Handbook: A Companion to Hope*. London: Black Swan, 2010.

_____. "Federalist Paper #51." *Our Documents—Interstate Commerce Act (1887)*. Accessed November 30, 2018. https://www.ourdocuments.gov/doc.php?doc=10&page=transcript.

Feinberg, Charles Lee. *The Prophecy of Ezekiel: The Glory of the Lord*. Chicago, IL: Moody Press, 1969.

Gaebelein, Arno Clemens. *Will There Be a Millennium? When and How? The Coming Reign of Christ in the Light of the Old and New Testaments.* New York: Publication Office "Our Hope", 1943.

Gilder, George F. *The Israel Test.* Minneapolis, MN: Richard Vigilante Books, 2009.

Glaser, Mitch, and Zhava Glaser. *The Fall Feasts of Israel.* Chicago: Moody Press, 1987. 206–07.

Glerup, Michael. *Ancient Christian Commentary on Scripture.* By Stevenson Kenneth. Vol. XIII. Downers Grove, Ill: InterVarsity Press, 2008.

GotQuestions.org, "What Does It Mean That Jesus Is the Son of David?" GotQuestions.org. Accessed June 18, 2017. https://www.gotquestions.org/Jesus-son-of-David.html.

GotQuestions.org. "What Is Good Biblical Exegesis?" GotQuestions.org. February 21, 2018. Accessed December 02, 2018. https://www.gotquestions.org/Biblical-exegesis.html.

Graham, Billy. *The Holy Spirit: Activating God's Power in Your Life.* Waco: Word Books, 1978.

Hedges, Chris. "'What Every Person Should Know About War.'" *New York Times.* July 06, 2003. Accessed July 05, 2015. http://www.nytimes.com/2003/07/06/books/chapters/0713-1st-hedges.html.

Hitchcock, Mark. *The End: A Complete Overview of Bible Prophecy and the End of Days.* Carol Stream, IL: Tyndale House Publishers, 2012.

Hitchcock, Mark._*101 Answers to the Most Asked Questions About the End Times.* Colorado Springs CO, Multnomah Publishers, 2001.

Ice, Thomas D. "What Is Replacement Theology?" Digital Commons@Liberty University. Accessed April 17, 2017. https://digitalcommons.liberty.edu/pretrib_arch/106/.

Ice, Thomas. Literal Sacrifices in the Millennium. *Pre-Trib Perspectives*, Accessed December 21, 2014. http://www.pre-trib.org/articles/view/literal-sacrifices-in-millennium

Jamieson, Robert, A. R. Fausset, and David Brown. *Commentary, Practical and Explanatory, on the Whole Bible.* Grand Rapids, MI: Zondervan, 1968.

Jeet Heer. "The New Utopians: Kim Stanley Robinson and the novelists who want to build a better future through science fiction" *New Republic*, November 9, 2015.

Jeffrey, Grant R. *Triumphant Return: The Coming Kingdom of God.* Toronto, Ont.: Frontier Research Publications, 2001.

_____. "Kansas State University." *Zika Virus Research at Biosecurity Research Institute Aims to Control, Fight Mosquitoes* | Kansas State University | News and Communications Services. Accessed November 29, 2018. https://www.k-state.edu/media/newsreleases/landonlect/harveytext903.html.

Kapur, Akash. "The Return of the Utopians." *The New Yorker.* June 19, 2017. Accessed December 01, 2018. https://www.newyorker.com/magazine/2016/10/03/the-return-of-the-utopians.

Keil, Carl Friedrich, and Franz Delitzsch. *Commentary on the Old Testament.* Isaiah. Vol. 7. Peabody, MA: Hendrickson Publishers, 1996.

Keller, Timothy J. "The Gospel in All Its Forms," *Leadership Journal* 29, no. 2. Spring 2008.

Keller, Timothy. *The Reason for God: Belief in an Age of Skepticism.* New York: Dutton Press, 2008.

Lewis, C. S. *Made for Heaven: And Why on Earth It Matters.* New York: HarperSanFrancisco, 2005.

_____. "Life Expectancy." World Health Organization. Accessed May 09, 2015. http://www.who.int/gho/mortality_burden_disease/life_tables/situation_trends_text/en/.

Liu, Joseph. "The Size and Distribution of the World's Christian Population." *Pew Research Center's Religion & Public Life Project.* September 27, 2018. Accessed November 30, 2018. http://www.pewforum.org/2011/12/19/global-christianity-exec/.

Lowrey, Annie. "Does Every Murder in the United States Really Cost Society $17 Million?" *Slate* magazine. October 21, 2010.

Accessed May 9, 2015. http://www.slate.com/articles/arts/everyday_economics/2010/10/true_crime_costs.html.

Lucado, Max. *Cast of Characters: Common People in the Hands of an Uncommon God*. Nashville, TN: Thomas Nelson, 2008.

Lugt, Herbert Vander. *The Daniel Papers: Daniel's Prophecy of 70 Weeks*. Grand Rapids: RBC Ministries, 2002.

MacArthur, John. *The MacArthur New Testament Commentary*, Vol. 3. Chicago: Moody Publishers, 1988.

MacArthur, John. *The Glory of Heaven: The Truth about Heaven, Angels, and Eternal Life, with New Material Addressing the Current Debate and Issues*. Wheaton, IL: Crossway, 2013.

MacArthur, John. *The MacArthur New Testament Commentary*. Vol. 17. Chicago, IL: Moody Press, 1984.

Madison, James. "Founders Online: Political Observations, 20 April 1795." National Archives and Records Administration. Accessed December 02, 2018. https://founders.archives.gov/documents/Madison/01-15-02-0423.

Manton, Thomas. *The Complete Works of Thomas Manton*, 123. London: James Nisbet and Company, 1873. http://www.puritanlibrary.com/, Internet. Accessed August 16, 2012.

March, Daniel. *Our Father's House, Or the Unwritten Word*. Philadelphia, PA: Ziegler & McCurdy, 1871.

Mathewson, Steven D. Risen: *50 Reasons Why the Resurrection Changed Everything*. Grand Rapids, MI: Baker Books, 2013.

McClain, Alva J. *The Greatness of the Kingdom: An Inductive Study of the Kingdom of God*. Winona Lake, IN: BMH Books, 1959.

Molica, Massimo C. "Continuity and Discontinuity Between the Millennial Kingdom and the Eternal State." CiteSeerX. Accessed December 02, 2018. http://citeseerx.ist.psu.edu/viewdoc/summary?doi=10.1.1.576.9681.

Nancy.cao. "United Nations Office on Drugs and Crime." *Integrity in the Criminal Justice System*. Accessed November 29, 2018. http://www.unodc.org/unodc/en/frontpage/2013/

November/new-unodc-se-asia-regional-programme-addresses-transnational-organized-crime-and-downsides-of-regional-integration.html.

Novak, Michael, and Jana Novak. *Washington's God: Religion, Liberty, and the Father of Our Country.* New York: BasicBooks, 2007.

_____. "November 2012." *The WellOften Reader.* Accessed December 16, 2016. http://wellandoftenpress.com/reader/to-be-vulnerable-and-fearless-an-interview-with-writer-warsan-shire/.

Oakes, Edward T. "Original Sin: A Disputation | Edward T. Oakes." *First Things.* November 01, 1998. Accessed December 02, 2018. https://www.firstthings.com/article/1998/11/001-original-sin-a-disputation.

Packer, J. I. *Concise Theology: A Guide to Historic Christian Beliefs.* Nottingham: Inter-Varsity Press, 2011.

Packer, J. I. *Rediscovering Holiness: Know the Fullness of Life with God.* Grand Rapids, MI: BakerBooks, a Division of Baker Publishing Group, 2009.

Pentecost, J. Dwight. *Things to Come: A Study in Biblical Eschatology.* Grand Rapids, MI: Zondervan, 1964.

Price, Randall. *The Temple and Bible Prophecy.* Eugene, OR.: Harvest House Publishers, 2005.

Ralph H. *The Expositor's Bible Commentary - Isaiah - Ezekiel: With the New International Version of the Holy Bible.* By Frank E. Gaebelein. Grand Rapids: Zondervan Pub. House, 1986.

Reid, David R. "Two Future Temples." *Growing Christians Ministries.* Accessed December 28, 2014. http://deeperwalk.lefora.com/topic/4207843/Does-Ez4047-Zerubbabels-temple-Jesus-Millennial-temple#.VKBwsCcA.

Shah, Anup. "World Military Spending." - *Global Issues.* Accessed May 09, 2015. http://www.globalissues.org/article/75/world-military-spending.

Spurgeon, C. H. *The Treasury of David.* London: Passmore and Alabaster, 1907.

Stumpf, Samuel Enoch., and James Fieser. *Socrates to Sartre: A History of Philosophy*. Boston, MA: McGraw-Hill, 1975.

Tabash, Edward. "What Population Stabilization Requires: Restrict Annual Immigration to the U.S." *Free Inquiry*, August 1, 2004.

_____. "The Beauty of God." *Edwards and the Bible: Christ, the Scope of Scripture* | Union Resources. Accessed December 05, 2016. https://www.uniontheology.org/resources/doctrine/god/the-beauty-of-god#_ftn1.

"The Cost of Crime." Amazon. January 01, 1901. Accessed July 15, 2019. https://www.amazon.com/cost-crime-Eugene-Smith/dp/B008O0XGG8.

_____. "The Glory of God as the Goal of History." Desiring God. November 29, 2018. Accessed November 29, 2018. https://www.desiringgod.org/articles/the-glory-of-god-as-the-goal-of-history.

The Macarthur Study Bible New American Standard Bible. Nelson Bibles, 2014.

_____. "4. The Millennial Kingdom and the Eternal State." | Bible.org. Accessed July 15, 2019. https://bible.org/seriespage/4-millennial-kingdom-and-eternal-state.

_____. "There's a Great Big Beautiful Tomorrow." Wikipedia. August 09, 2018. Accessed November 30, 2018. https://en.wikipedia.org/wiki/There%27s_a_Great_Big_Beautiful_Tomorrow.

_____. "Top 10 Worst Things In Nature." Despadani. Accessed November 29, 2018. http://despadanicom.blogspot.com/2011/03/top-10-worst-things-in-nature.html.

_____."Thou Hast Made Us for Thyself, O Lord …" – St. Augustine." Catholicism Pure & Simple. August 28, 2014. Accessed July 15, 2019. https://catholicismpure.wordpress.com/2014/08/28/thou-hast-made-us-for-thyself-o-lord-st-augustine/.

_____. "Utopia." *Merriam-Webster*. Accessed December 01, 2018. https://www.merriam-webster.com/dictionary/utopia.

_____. "Utopia." Wikipedia. Accessed September 23, 2010. https://en.wikipedia.org/wiki/Utopia.

Walvoord, John F. "The Nations In The Millennium And The Eternal State." Bible.org. Accessed January 2, 2016. https://bible.org/seriespage/15-nations-Millennium-and-eternal-state.

Walvoord, John F. *End Times: Understanding Today's World Events in Biblical Prophecy*. Nashville: Word Pub., 1998.

Walvoord, John F. *The Millennial Kingdom: A Basic Text in Premillennial Theology*. Grand Rapids : Zondervan, 1983: Academie Books.

Walvoord, John F. *The Revelation of Jesus Christ*. Accessed May 19, 2006. http://Theologicalstudies.Org/Files/Resources/Mollica_Millennium_And_Eternal_State_2.Pdf

West, Nathaniel. "Part 1 *The Thousand Years in Both Testaments.*" *In The Thousand Year Reign of Christ: The Classic Work on the Millennium*. Grand Rapids, MI: Kregel Publications, 1993.

Westminster Shorter Catechism. Accessed December 01, 2018. https://reformed.org/documents/wsc/index.html?_top=https%3A%2F%2Freformed.org%2Fdocuments%2FWSC.html.

_____. "What Is God's Glory?" Desiring God. Accessed December 7, 2016. http://www.desiringgod.org/interviews/what-is-god-s-glory.

_____. "What Is Progressive Sanctification?" GotQuestions.org. Accessed January 1, 2017. https://www.gotquestions.org/progressive-sanctification.html.

_____. "Will Christ Reign Forever?" *Christian Courier*. Accessed October 11, 2016. https://www.christiancourier.com/articles/466-will-christ-reign-forever.

_____. "World Military Spending." - Global Issues. Accessed July 15, 2019. http://www.globalissues.org/article/75/world-military-spending.

Whitcomb, John. *Romans Chapter 6*. Accessed December 02, 2018. http://www.middletownbiblechurch.org/proph/templemi.htm.

Whitcomb, John. *The Millennial Temple of Ezekiel 40–48*. Accessed December 02, 2018. http://www.middletownbiblechurch.org/proph/templemi.htm

Wiersbe, Warren W. "Romans." In *Wiersbe's Expository Outlines on the New Testament.* Wheaton, IL: Victor Books, 1992.

Yun, and Paul Hattaway. *The Heavenly Man: The Remarkable True Story of Chinese Christian Brother Yun*. Peabody, MA: Hendrickson Publishers, 2009.

Endnotes

1 "Paul Harvey Landon Lecture, September 19, 2003," Kansas State University Media Relations, accessed December 21, 2014, https://www.k-state.edu/media/newsreleases/landonlect/harveytext903.html.

2 Akash Kapur, "The Return of the Utopians," *The New Yorker*, June 19, 2017, accessed December 1, 2018, https://www.newyorker.com/magazine/2016/10/03/the-return-of-the-utopians.

3 Jeet Heer, "The New Utopians: Kim Stanley Robinson and the Novelists Who Want to Build a Better Future Through Science Fiction," *New Republic*, November 9, 2015, accessed July 1, 2019, https://newrepublic.com/ article/123217/new-utopians.

4 Don Moen, "Let Your Glory Fall" (Brentwood: Integrity Music, 1997).

5 Paul N. Benware, *Understanding End times Prophecy: A Comprehensive Approach* (Chicago: Moody Publishers, 2006), 25.

6 John MacArthur, *The Macarthur Study Bible New American Standard Bible* (Nashville: Nelson Bibles, 2014), 1083.

7 For a summary of basic guidelines for biblical interpretation, read "What Is Good Biblical Exegesis?" GotQuestions.org, https://www.gotquestions.org/Biblical-exegesis.html.

8 Arno Clemens Gaebelein, *Will There Be a Millennium? When and How? The Coming Reign of Christ in the Light of the Old and New Testaments* (New York: Publication Office "Our Hope," 1943), 19.

9 Thomas Manton, *The Complete Works of Thomas Manton*, vol. XIII (London: James Nisbet and Company, 1873), 122.

10 The Edenic Covenant, also called the Adamic Covenant (Genesis 1:26–30; 2:16–17), the Noahic Covenant (Genesis 9), the Abrahamic Covenant (Genesis 12:1–3, 6–7; 13:14–17; 15; 17:1–14; 22:15–18), the Palestinian Covenant, also called the Land Covenant (Deuteronomy 30:1–10), the

Mosaic Covenant (Deuteronomy 11; et al.), the Davidic Covenant (2 Samuel 7:8–16), the New Covenant (Jeremiah 31:31–34).

11 Mitch Glaser and Zhava Glaser, *The Fall Feasts of Israel* (Chicago: Moody Press, 1987), 206–07.

12 Mark Hitchcock, *The End: A Complete Overview of Bible Prophecy and the End of Days.* (Carol Stream, IL: Tyndale House Publishers, 2012), 89.

13 In verses 38–45 the psalmist concludes that God had not kept His covenant with David because the current king had been defeated. However, God's chastening of the nation did not mean that He had rejected Israel forever, but only for a season, in order that they might be disciplined for their disobedience.

14 "The Glory of God as the Goal of History," John Piper, *Desiring God*, 1976, accessed August 10, 2012. https://www.desiringgod.org/articles/the-glory-of-god-as-the-goal-of-history.

15 J. I. Packer, *Rediscovering Holiness: Know the Fullness of Life with God* (Grand Rapids: BakerBooks, 2009), 65.

16 "Next Year in Jerusalem," Michele Alperin, *My Jewish Learning*, accessed December 01, 2018. https://www.myjewishlearning.com/article/next-year-in-jerusalem/.

17 In Revelation 9:1–2 John describes black smoke, "like the smoke of a great furnace" billowing from the pit when it is opened. Some interpreters believe the Abyss is the same as Tartarus mentioned in 2 Peter 2:4 (translated "hell" in the King James Version)where Scripture says some of the angels who participated in Satan's rebellion in heaven have been confined as they await the final judgment. Jude 6 adds that these fallen angels are presently enchained there. If Tartarus is indeed the same as the Abyss, it is a "holding cell" as well as a place of punishment (fire). In any case, Satan will be incarcerated there during the Millennium.

18 Martin Luther, "A Mighty Fortress Is Our God," Frederick H. Hedge, trans., William Henry Furness, 1802–1896, and Moritz Retzsch. *Gems of German Verse* (Philadelphia: Willis P. Hazard, 1851), 93.

19 John F. Walvoord, *End Times: Understanding Today's World Events in Biblical Prophecy* (Nashville: Word Publishing, 1998), 163.

20 John F. Walvoord, *The Millennial Kingdom: A Basic Text in Premillennial Theology* (Grand Rapids: Zondervan Publishing House, 1983), 289.

21 MacArthur, The Macarthur Study Bible New American Standard Bible, 1410.

22 Isaac Watts, "Joy to the World," *Psalms of David Imitated in the Language of the New Testament* (London: T. Longman [etc.], 1769), 209.

23 Davies Gilbert, "The First Nowell," *Christmas Carols Ancient and Modern*, by William B. Sandys and Davies Gilbert (London: Richard Beckley, 1833), 13.

24 Charles Wesley, George Whitefield, "Hark! The Herald Angels Sing," *A Collection of Hymns for Social Worship* (London: William Strahan, 1753).

25 Edmund H. Sears, "It Came Upon a Midnight Clear," *The Christian Register* Volume 28, Number 52, (Boston: December 29, 1849), 206.

26 Placide Cappeau, Adolphe C. Adam, *O Holy Night*, John Sullivan Dwight, trans., (New York: G. Schirmer, 1858).

27 "We Three Kings," John H. Hopkins, *Carols, Hymns and Songs* (New York: Church Book Depository, 1863), 12–13.

28 George Frideric Handel, *Messiah*, Part I, Scene 3: "The Prophecy of Christ's Birth", Movement 12 "For Unto Us a Child is Born" (London, 1741).

29 James Montgomery, "Angels from the Realms of Glory", *Christian Psalmist* (Glasgow: Chalmers and Collins, 1825), 389–390.

30 Keith Getty and Stuart Townend, *O Church, Arise*, (Brentwood: Thankyou Music, 2005).

31 Robert Jamieson, A. R. Fausset, and David Brown, *Commentary, Practical and Explanatory, on the Whole Bible* (Grand Rapids: Zondervan, 1968), 1590.

32 Isaac Watts, "Joy to the World," 1769.

33 Nathaniel West, *The Thousand Year Reign of Christ: The Classic Work on the Millennium*, (Grand Rapids: Kregel Publications, 1993), 306.

34 MacArthur, The Macarthur Study Bible New American Standard Bible, 1083.

35 Carl Friedrich Keil and Franz Delitzsch, *Commentary on the Old Testament. Isaiah. Vol. 7* (Peabody, MA: Hendrickson Publishers, 1996), 324–25.

36 Will Durant and Ariel Durant, *Lessons of History* (New York: Simon & Schuster, 2010), 22.

37 "Top 10 Worst Things In Nature," J. Frater, Your History Haven.com, accessed November 29, 2018. http://yourhistoryhaven.com/2016/06/top-10-worst-things-in-nature/.

38 Eugene Smith, *The Cost of Crime* (Washington, DC: U.S. State Department, 1901), 11.

39 "Integrity in the Criminal Justice System," Nancy Cao, United Nations Office on Drugs and Crime, accessed May 9, 2015. http://www.unodc.org/unodc/en/frontpage/2013/November/

new-unodc-se-asia-regional-programme-addresses-transnational-organized-crime-and-downsides-of-regional-integration.html.

40 "The Aggregate Burden of Crime," David A. Anderson, *SpringerLink*, January 31, 1999, accessed May 9, 2015. http://dx.doi.org/10.2139/ssrn.147911.

41 "Does Every Murder in the United States Really Cost Society $17 Million?," Annie Lowrey, *Slate* magazine, October 21, 2010. accessed May 9, 2015. http://www.slate.com/articles/arts/everyday_economics/2010/10/true_crime_costs.html.

42 James Madison, "Political Observations," April 20, 1795, *Letters and Other Writings of James Madison, Vol. 4*, 1865, 491.

43 "What Every Person Should Know About War," Chris Hedges, *New York Times*, July 06, 2003. accessed July 05, 2015. http://www.nytimes.com/2003/07/06/books/chapters/0713-1st-hedges.html.

44 "What Every Person Should Know About War."

45 "World Military Spending," Anup Shah, *Global Issues*, accessed May 09, 2015. http://www.globalissues.org/article/75/world-military-spending.

46 "Life Expectancy," World Health Organization, Global Health Observatory Data), accessed May 09, 2015. http://www.who.int/gho/mortality_burden_disease/life_tables/situation_trends_text/en/.

47 James Madison, "Federalist Paper #51", *Independent Journal*, February 6, 1788, *Constitution Society*, accessed July 1, 2019, https://www.constitution.org/fed/federa51.htm.

48 John MacArthur, *The MacArthur New Testament Commentary, Vol 3, Matthew 16–23* (Chicago: Moody Publishers, 1988), 348.

49 Anthony C. Thiselton, *The First Epistle to the Corinthians. The New International Greek Testament Commentary* (Grand Rapids: Eerdmans, 2000), 1232.

50 Herbert Vander Lugt, *The Daniel Papers: Daniel's Prophecy of 70 Weeks* (Grand Rapids: RBC Ministries, 2002), 10.

51 Joseph Dillow, *Destiny: The Future Reign of the Servant Kings*, Conroe: Grace Theology Press, 2018), 955.

52 Paul Hattaway. *The Heavenly Man: The Remarkable True Story of Chinese Christian Brother Yun* (Peabody, MA: Hendrickson Publishers, 2009), 14.

53 George F. Gilder, *The Israel Test* (Minneapolis: Richard Vigilante Books, 2009), 3.

54 "The Nations in the Millennium and the Eternal State," John F. Walvoord, Bible.org, accessed January 2, 2016. https://bible.org/seriespage/15-nations-Millennium-and-eternal-state.

55 Edward Snyder, Lawrence Kusik, Nino Rota, "A Time for Us (Love Theme from *Romeo & Juliet*)." (New York: Sony/ATV Music Publishing LLC, 1969).

56 John Lennon, "Imagine." *Imagine*, track 1. (Ascot, Berkshire: Ascot Sound Studios, 1971).

57 John MacArthur, *The MacArthur New Testament Commentary, Vol. 17, John 12–21* (Chicago, IL: Moody Press, 1984), 434.

58 In Romans 8:23 Paul refers to this transformation as "the redemption of our body." God redeemed your soul at the moment you were born again. Your physical body's redemption is yet to come.

59 J. I. Packer, *Concise Theology: A Guide to Historic Christian Beliefs*, (Nottingham: Inter-Varsity Press, 2011), 254–256.

60 C. S. Lewis, *Made for Heaven: And Why on Earth It Matters* (New York: HarperSanFrancisco, 2005), Xi.

61 Robert Robinson, "Come Thou Fount of Every Blessing," *A Collection of Hymns Used by the Church of Christ in Angel Alley, Bishopsgate*, (London, 1759), 2–3.

62 In Jesus' Parable of the Ten Minas (Luke 19:11–27), the master grants authority over various numbers of cities as repayment for profitable investments by his servants. This parable encourages faithfulness to Christ in the present life by providing indication of how Christ will reward His people when we reign with Him in the Millennium.

63 Randy C. Alcorn, *Heaven* (Carol Stream: Tyndale House Publishers, 2008), 350.

64 John MacArthur, *The Glory of Heaven: The Truth about Heaven, Angels, and Eternal Life*, (Wheaton, IL: Crossway, 2013), 138.

65 Lewis, *Made for Heaven*, 47–48.

66 "The Size and Distribution of the World's Christian Population," Joseph Liu, *Pew Research Center's Religion & Public Life Project*, September 27, 2018, accessed November 30, 2018. http://www.pewforum.org/2011/12/19/global-christianity-exec/.

67 "The Millennial Kingdom and the Eternal State," John F. Walvoord, Bible.org, accessed November 30, 2018. https://bible.org/seriespage/4-millennial-kingdom-and-eternal-state.

68 Lewis Sperry Chafer and John F. Walvoord, *Major Bible Themes: 52 Vital Doctrines of the Scripture Simplified and Explained* (Grand Rapids: Zondervan, 1974), 357.

69 Randall Price, *The Temple and Bible Prophecy* (Eugene, OR: Harvest House Publishers, 2005), 531.

70 C. H. Spurgeon, *The Treasury of David* (London: Passmore and Alabaster, 1907), 342.

71 John MacArthur, The Macarthur Study Bible New American Standard Bible, 816.

72 "Bethlehem's Supernatural Star," John Piper, *Desiring God*, accessed July 1, 2019. https://www.desiringgod.org/articles/bethlehems-supernatural-star.

73 Alfred Edersheim, the noted Jewish authority on the temple, allows that Ezekiel's Temple may be "prophetic"—that is, understood literally (*The Temple: Its Ministry and Services*, 1995), 263.

74 Michael Glerup, *Ancient Christian Commentary on Scripture, Volume XIII* (Downers Grove, IL: InterVarsity Press, 2008), 125–27.

75 "Literal Sacrifices in the Millennium," Thomas Ice, *Pre-Trib Perspectives*, accessed December 21, 2014. http://www.pre-trib.org/articles/view/literal-sacrifices-in-millennium.

76 Max Lucado, *Cast of Characters: Common People in the Hands of an Uncommon God* (Nashville: Thomas Nelson, 2008), 3.

77 Lamar Eugene Cooper, *The New American Commentary: An Exegetical and Theological Exposition of Holy Scripture, Volume 17, John 12–21* (Nashville: B & H Publishing Group, 1994), 391.

78 "Two Future Temples." David R. Reid, *Growing Christians Ministries*, accessed December 28, 2014. http://deeperwalk.lefora.com/topic/4207843/Does-Ez4047-Zerubbabels-temple-Jesus-Millennial-temple#.VKBwsCcA.

79 "The Millennial Temple of Ezekiel 40–48," John Whitcomb, accessed December 02, 2018. http://www.middletownbiblechurch.org/proph/templemi.htm

80 Charles Lee Feinberg, *The Prophecy of Ezekiel: The Glory of the Lord* (Chicago: Moody Press, 1969), 234.

81 Chafer and Walvoord, *Major Bible Themes*, 358.

82 Price, *The Temple and Bible Prophecy*, 549.

83 R. H. Alexander, *The Expositor's Bible Commentary, Volume 6 Isaiah, Jeremiah, Lamentations, Ezekiel* (Grand Rapids: Zondervan Publishing House, 1986), 949.

84 For a detailed analysis of the differences in regulations and rituals connected with the temple of the Mosaic Law and millennial temple, see J. Dwight Pentecost, *Things to Come: A Study in Biblical Eschatology*, Zondervan, 1958, 518–531.

85 For a detailed explanation of this interpretation, see Charles Feinberg, *The Prophecy of Ezekiel*, Moody Press, 1969. 198–199.
86 Feinberg, *The Prophecy of Ezekiel*, 258.
87 Cooper, *The New American Commentary*, 390.
88 For a good summary of the various views on this question see, Molica, Massimo C., "Continuity and Discontinuity Between the Millennial Kingdom and the Eternal State," http://citeseerx.ist.psu.edu/viewdoc/summary?doi=10.1.1.576.9681.
89 Isaac Asimov, *The Universe: From Flat Earth to Quasar* (New York: Avon, 1966), 15.
90 Kenneth Boa and Robert M. Bowman Jr., *Sense and Nonsense about Heaven and Hell* (Grand Rapids: Zondervan, 2007), 165.
91 "Concluding Revelations And Exhortations," John F. Walvoord, Walvoord.com, Accessed July 1, 2019. https://walvoord.com/book/export/html/280
92 Easley and Anders, *Holman New Testament Commentary*, 395.
93 "Will Christ Reign Forever?" Wayne Jackson, *Christian Courier*. Accessed October 11, 2016. https://www.christiancourier.com/articles/466-will-christ-reign-forever.
94 Alva J. McClain, *The Greatness of the Kingdom: An Inductive Study of the Kingdom of God* (Winona Lake: BMH Books, 1959), 513.
95 McClain, *The Greatness of the Kingdom*, 513.
96 Jamieson, Fausset, and Brown, *Commentary, Practical and Explanatory, on the Whole Bible*, 1222.
97 Steven D. Mathewson, *Risen: 50 Reasons Why the Resurrection Changed Everything* (Grand Rapids: Baker Books, 2013), 116.
98 Billy Graham, *The Holy Spirit: Activating God's Power in Your Life* (Waco: Word Books, 1978), 7.
99 Grant R. Jeffrey, *Triumphant Return: The Coming Kingdom of God* (Toronto: Frontier Research Publications, 2001), 159.
100 West, *The Thousand Year Reign of Christ*, 1.
101 Samuel Enoch Stumpf and James Fieser, *Socrates to Sartre: A History of Philosophy*, (Boston: McGraw-Hill, 1975), 60.
102 Daniel March, *Our Father's House, Or the Unwritten Word* (Philadelphia: Ziegler & McCurdy, 1871), 559.
103 "What Is God's Glory?" John Piper, *Desiring God*, accessed December 7, 2016. http://www.desiringgod.org/interviews/what-is-god-s-glory.
104 Niall Edworthy, Cramsie Petra, and Emily Faccini, *The Optimist's Handbook: A Companion to Hope*, (New York: Free Press, 2008), 16.

105 "The Beauty of God," Steve DeWitt, *Union Resources*, accessed December 05, 2016. https://www.uniontheology.org/resources/doctrine/god/the-beauty-of-god#_ftn1.

106 Mathewson, *Risen*, 16.

107 Lewis, *Made for Heaven*, 85–86.

108 Lewis, *Made for Heaven*, 62.

109 Timothy Keller, *The Reason for God: Belief in an Age of Skepticism* (New York: Dutton Press, 2008), 133–35.

110 Lewis, *Made for Heaven*, 63.

111 "To Be Vulnerable and Fearless: An Interview with Writer Warsan Shire," Kameelah Janan Rasheed, *The Well and Often Reader*, November 2012, accessed December 16, 2016. http://wellandoftenpress.com/reader/to-be-vulnerable-and-fearless-an-interview-with-writer-warsan-shire/.

112 "Original Sin: A Disputation," Edward T. Oakes, *First Things*, November 01, 1998, accessed December 02, 2018. https://www.firstthings.com/article/1998/11/001-original-sin-a-disputation.

113 Warren W. Wiersbe, *Wiersbe's Expository Outlines on the New Testament*, (Wheaton: Victor Books, 1992), 388.

114 Wiersbe, Wiersbe's Expository Outlines on the New Testament, 388.

115 West, *The Thousand Year Reign of Christ*, 260.

116 Jeffrey, *Triumphant Return*, 46.

117 Richard M. Sherman, Robert B. Sherman, *There's a Great Big Beautiful Tomorrow*, (Burbank: Wonderland Music Company, 1963).

118 "Shorter Catechism of the Assembly of Divines: The 1647 Westminster Confession and Subordinate Documents," C. Matthew McMahon, *A Puritan's Mind*, accessed December 01, 2018. https://reformed.org/documents/wsc/index.html?_top=https%3A%2F%2Freformed.org%2Fdocuments%2FWSC. html.

119 Wikipedia. "Utopia." Last modified June 5, 2019. accessed July 1, 2019. https://en.wikipedia.org/wiki/Utopia.

120 Packer, *Concise Theology*, 266–67.

Printed in the United States
By Bookmasters